THE SILENT TRAVELLER
IN LONDON

IN MEMORY

OF

the death of my beloved brother, without whose help in
bringing me up I should never have been able to see this
amazing world in its age of progress and destruction,
fighting side by side;

and also

IN MEMORY

OF

the entrance of the invader into my native city, Kiukiang,
on July 25th, 1938

THE SILENT TRAVELLER
IN LONDON

碎襟敦倫

BY

CHIANG YEE

Author of *The Silent Traveller in Lakeland*, of *The Chinese Eye*
and of *Chinese Calligraphy*

LONDON: COUNTRY LIFE LTD
2-10 *Tavistock Street, Covent Garden, W.C.2*
NEW YORK: TRANSATLANTIC ARTS INC.

First published in 1938
by Country Life Limited
Tavistock Street, London, W.C.2
Printed in Great Britain by
Lowe & Brydone Printers Ltd,
London, N.W.10
Eighth impression 1951

Contents

v

List of Plates

Introduction

Anyone who chanced to read my book on the English Lakeland, would never imagine me writing anything about London, as I claimed there to find that living under London fogs had its unpleasant side. I wrote the truth. But nevertheless a reasonable person finds some kind of beauty everywhere. When I stay in London I grow at times very tired of it and at others very fond of it. I have seen many beautiful things in London and certainly made a great many curious reflections on all I saw since I came here five years ago. As I am an Oriental (actually one of those strange Chinese people who "belong to an age gone by," as a London critic said of me) I am bound to look at many things from a different angle. But is it really so different? I very much doubt it myself, but my readers shall judge for themselves. I have never agreed with people who hold that the various nationalities differ greatly from each other. They may be different superficially, but they eat, drink, sleep, dress, and shelter themselves from wind and rain in the same way. In particular their outlook on life need not vary fundamentally. Individual thought is always individual, and similarity of tastes will always link people without regard for any geographical boundary. You would expect your butcher to think of a frisky young lamb as good to eat, not to look at! A Chinese butcher will think the same as he does!

It always gives me pleasure to jot down my impressions of anything I have seen, and this book on London has been in my mind for quite a long time, but I still feel ashamed to give it form so soon. I quite agree with my friends who tell me that the first impression is always the most fresh and lively. But then one is apt to find later that the first impression was false. Before I came to London, I often heard stories of it from people who had travelled there, or read of it in papers and books; but those accounts were much too general and could bring no clear picture before my mind. I suppose people who hear and read about China must suffer in the same way. Many travellers who have gone to China for only a few months come back and write books about it, including everything from literature and philosophy to domestic and social life, and economic conditions. And some have written without having been there at all. I can only admire their temerity and their skill in generalising on great questions. I expect I suffer together with many others in the world, whose characters have been mis-generalised in some way. I was thought to be a Communist by an English friend because, he declared, all young Chinese were Communists; and another criticised me as a die-hard or one belonging to an age gone by. I was only casually acquainted with them. I can imagine there must be a good number of people who still wonder why I have no pig-tail on my head, or who think I must be the same sort of person as Mr. Wu or Charlie Chan!

A modest person with little ability, who dares not make generalisations on big topics, I would like first of all to advise my readers not to expect from me anything approaching an historical or academic study of London. There are heaps of books written by well-known historians, scholars, and artists, both English and foreign, which deal with all the great features of this city. They are the classics of London; but mine is a book of another sort. As I am diffident of fixing my eyes on big things, I generally glance down on the small ones. There are a great many tiny events which it has given me great joy to look at, to watch, and to think about. And as they are so tiny, other people may have neglected them. This little book can perhaps be called a collection of odds and ends of observations, which may amuse a few people at bedtime or in idle moments after tea or dinner. Though I am going to put some order into my impressions presently, I would like to give the reader some free samples here, like the sweet- or the biscuit-seller. They are the very first observations I can remember. I travelled on a French boat from Shanghai to France. After staying one night in Paris, I came to London. The first thing I saw after Dover was chimney-pot after chimney-pot on both sides of the railway. The nearer I got into town, the more pots I saw. At that time I thought I was coming to a pot-making factory. Then I was met by a fellow-countryman at Victoria Station and he took me to a Chinese restaurant. As soon as we got into the lift of a tube station, I saw an elderly labourer vigorously scolding a handsome young man who was running into the lift by the wrong gate. Although the first had a dirty face and hands as if he had just come out of a coal-bunker, yet he showed much more respect for the common law than the other in his flashy suit. I was deeply impressed and puzzled at this proceeding, though I suppose Londoners hardly notice such things. Only a few days later, I was waiting for a bus in front of the Dominion Theatre at Tottenham Court Road. As soon as the bus stopped, a crowd of people tried to rush into it. Suddenly I saw a young boy stopping a middle-aged man who wanted to squeeze in before the other passengers could get off. Although the man struggled, the boy pulled him back forcibly until all the passengers had cleared out of the way. I was so struck by the event, that I forgot to get on to the bus myself. I must say that the elderly labourer and the young boy would be very rarely seen in large Chinese towns, and to both of them I pay a high respect. I am sure none of our people would have put themselves out to that extent, although they might have felt the same about it. Such actions are a great help to conductors and policemen!

I wonder whether this sort of remark will entertain readers at all; I am certainly not attempting to please learned scholars! I remember once talking with a lady who told me she would never write a book on "oddments" for the sake of amusement, for no scholar would do that kind of thing! It is interesting to know that scholars are the same all over the world, for there are plenty of Chinese who would agree with her. Our thought in general is governed, as you probably know, by Confucian ideas. A subject unconnected with the Confucian virtues of right-eousness, filial piety, sincerity, etc., would not be discussed among scholars. If any book is published that has no concern with these things, one dare not even keep it in a study or highly valued room for fear of offending "the classics." The type of book which I am now writing would be called in Chinese a "book under pillow-case" or one "for the rest after tea or after wine." You may simply say it is a bedside book. As I am not able to write essays like Jonathan Swift's *Compliment to the Readers*, in which he divides readers into three classes, the *Superficial*, the *Ignorant*, and the *Learned*, and says he has with much felicity fitted his pen to the genius and advantage of each, I can only hope my readers will not complain too much of having been taken to see many negligible things in London.

I suppose most people who know anything about Chinese food have heard the expression "Chop Suey." Since I came to London, I have frequently invited my English friends to a Chinese meal. They generally choose "Chop

Suey" from the menu—as soon as they get it, they ask me what it is made of. I simply answer—"made of all things." All Chinese cooks and waiters know their English visitors like this dish. In Chinese it is called "Tsa Tsui," which in the Cantonese pronunciation sounds like "Chop Suey." "Tsa" means "mixed up" and "Tsui" "fragments"; the whole expression means "a mixture of everything." There are some nice pieces of meat and a fine assortment of vegetables in the dish, which has a strange composite flavour. Funnily enough it has become a special Chinese dish in the West now! After this explanation, perhaps I can call this book a "Chop Suey of London"; there is nothing of great value in it, but it may be appetising to some.

I am lucky enough to have lived in London during five important years in which big events have happened one after the other, such as the Silver Jubilee, the death of King George V, the Hoare crisis, the Abdication, the Coronation, the Bus Strike, the Eden crisis, etc. Such events only happen once in a lifetime. How lucky for an Oriental like me to have seen all these together in a short time! I myself have seen three kings *in the distance* and would on that account, have been thought a most reverend person if I had lived in the old days of China. Republican China is not much interested in such things.

I shall certainly not try to deal with politics, because I cannot understand them at all. During these five years it has seemed to me everyone in London can talk politics and can interpret them so well that I feel I must be a most stupid man. I appear to shock people when I answer them that I know nothing about politics. An old postman whom I have known for four years had a chat with me one evening when I was posting my letter at the pillar-box near my house. It was just after the invasion of Austria. He asked me what I thought of it and was puzzled when

I answered that I had no ideas on the subject. Then I said, "What do you think of the happenings in Abyssinia, Spain, and China?" He answered me very positively that he had plenty of ideas about them, but these three presented quite different problems. Many a person would think like him, and would argue with me vigorously if I declared they were one and the same. Everyone wants peace, so they say, but actually nearly everyone is at war or preparing for it. You can find the word "peace" a good number of times in the newspapers every day, but you will find the same number of "wars" there too. Abyssinians were to be civilised. Austrians were under the tyrannical control of Schuschnigg's regime. Lawless Chinese are to be put in order. I can only open my eyes wide in continual amazement at all these events! A young lady friend of mine came to tea with me three years ago and we talked of almost everything under the sun. She gave thorough approval to the Italians' action in "civilising" the Abyssinians, because she thought the latter were barbarians. I smiled at her without saying a word and said then, "What do you think of the Chinese?" She told me that we were highly civilised people and she hated our friendly neighbour doing anything against us. I was greatly flattered, but I could never agree with her that we are not barbarians. If so, why do most of our elders and even some of my contemporaries still think that Dutch, French, and English, indeed all Europeans are "foreign devils"? I think "barbarian" is not a bad name; it only depends on how it is defined. Actually we were called "barbarians" by Indians thousands of years ago. When our greatest monk, Hsüan-tsang, of T'ang dynasty (A.D. 618–905), went to India to learn Buddhism for many years, the monks of Nālandā considered him so much one of themselves that they wanted to dissuade him from returning to China:

"India," they said, "has seen the birth of Buddha, and although He has left the earth, His sacred traces still remain here. To visit them one after another, to adore them, and to sing His praises is the way to bring happiness to your life. Why come here to leave us all of a sudden? Besides, *China is a land of barbarians.* They have a scorn for monks and for faith. That is why Buddha did not will to be born there. The inhabitants' views are narrow, and their sins go deep. That is why the sages and saints (of India) have not gone there . . . .[1]

Although Hsüan-tsang's reply, from the pen of his biographer, is an outburst of national pride followed by the praises of Confucian traditionalism, humanitarianism, and humanism, yet I do not see why we should not be called "barbarians." I am perfectly sure that Egyptians must have called us "barbarians" five thousand years ago! The late Sir James S. Lockhart, who had been in the government of Hong Kong and Weihaiwei for nearly forty years, had a tremendous knowledge of Chinese studies. I used to visit him every Saturday morning before he became seriously ill, and he was a person of rich sense of humour. He always called himself a "foreign devil" with little knowledge, when he wanted me to explain a passage of Chinese for him. But he was so patriotic (I cannot find any better word for this), that he told me he almost crossed out every Chinese word "Yi" (which means "barbarian") in the Chinese texts in his collection. He had collected all the texts for *Gems of Chinese Literature*, translated by Prof. H. Giles, and had published them in Chinese through a Chinese publisher in Shanghai. Unfortunately, the word "Yi" occurred a good number of times in one long essay and he changed them all into my name "Yee" instead,

---

[1] From Réné Grousset's *In the Footsteps of the Buddha*, p. 199.

because these two words had the same sound. One day I took this book to him and said that I was a "barbarian." He roared with laughter and then explained that that must be the fault of my own compatriot who published it. Oh, that happy moment will be always in my memory until I see him in the next world!

This book is illustrated with my own drawings, which may also give it a different flavour from other books about London. After I had been here nearly a year, I began to try secretly to adapt my brush to the daily scene around me. I was warned by an English friend who had very good taste in Chinese paintings, that with my brush I should not succeed well in painting English scenery, even if I tried. He thought that I could not achieve my aim, and also that my original style of work would be spoiled by trying to do this. I was grateful for his interest, but was unwilling to give up the attempt. Although in three years I had many failures, yet those drawings reproduced in my book on the English lakes have been kindly received by readers. I am particularly grateful to those who criticised my drawings very frankly and told me which they liked and which they did not. I hope they will tell me what they think of the drawings reproduced here.

Further, most people nowadays know something about the general appearance and subject matter of Chinese paintings. Unfortunately, they are apt to be biassed. If they see a picture with one or two birds, a few trees or rocks piled together, they will certainly say that that is a lovely Chinese painting. But if they find anything like Western buildings or a modern figure there, they will suddenly say, "that is not Chinese." No matter if the manner of painting is good or not, they will probably ignore it. The difference between our paintings and yours is not in the subject matter, but in the medium we use. We paint birds, flowers, and landscapes from what we see around us. Although we do not paint directly from nature, we have to paint what we have once seen in nature. In this book I have painted from the surroundings in which I have lived these last few years, and I hope my readers will not be so biassed as to say that they do not like the paintings because they are not "Chinese." And I also hope some of my readers are not biassed in another way and will not say that they like this kind of painting because it has a Chinese flavour. I should like them to criticise my work without preconceptions.

There is one more point I would like to mention in this introduction. Probably, most Europeans do not realise what a state of mind we Chinese are in nowadays. I am not speaking here for myself only, but for all my fellow countrymen. "Inferiority complex" is a complaint from which probably any human being suffers in some degree. But to this merry-making country we have come from a very long distance, and we are bound to make some comparisons with our own nation. We know we have many weak points, but we believe we can put them right if we try and are given time. And after all, sweeping reforms are weighty problems for any country and cannot be achieved by one person or in a short period. The past history and the size of our country make them even more complex. Some of us find it very difficult to adapt ourselves to London life and keep apart in a dull way; some refuse to mix in circles where they would be asked many difficult questions arising from popular books and films on Chinese life. This is all due to "inferiority complex." Confucius says: "I will not be afflicted at men's not knowing me; I will be afflicted that I do not know men." This is why I myself have tried to know London well.

All the friends I have met here have been extremely

kind to me. Whenever we meet, they generally ask me whether I have had good news from home. But the news that we get is seldom good. Really, no news is good news for us! Apart from our internal troubles, we have a friendly neighbour who always insists on making friends with us whether we wish it or not. During these five years, any news that appeared in the papers always had something to do with this quarrel. It is interesting for the world to know that a young lady intends to marry an old man by making quarrels before they can really fall in love with each other. Perhaps there has never been a case like this in the history of the world! I can say nothing about this question for my part and do not want to say anything because I am "The Silent Traveller." Besides I have many other and different thoughts in my head. I have wandered about London very silently and really seen a good many things through my silence.

I once read in *The Times*, an article entitled "Silence in the Tube" in which it announced that the London Passenger Transport Board, which was constantly devising new plans for its customers' delight, had recently announced it was to spend a large sum in making part of its tube lines silent. "But this change," it continued, "from noisy trains with silent passengers to noisy passengers in silent trains, if it is accomplished, will be but another of the revolutions in the underground life of London which is perhaps particularly noticeable to the occasional visitor to the capital over the past twenty years." By this quotation I only want to illustrate that it is quite possible to be silent in London however much people may disbelieve it. And I must say that there is a very good point about being silent, namely, that you feel yourself more at leisure than others who are always filling up time with chatter. "Time" is the important factor in life, especially for people living in London. I would like to quote here a copy of the inscription on an old sundial which was kept by Miss C. M. N. Brooker:

> *Time is too slow for those who wait,*
> *Too swift for those who fear,*
> *Too long for those who grieve,*
> *Too short for those who rejoice:*
> *But for those who love Time is Eternity.*

The Silent Traveller might join the last group! This book is to be a sort of record of all the things I have talked over to myself during these five years in London, where I have been so silent.

PART I
London Scene

Spring in London

I have passed only thirty-five springs: the first ten slipped by without my notice, the second ten seemed to be gone before I knew how to enjoy them, the third ten gave me grief because, overburdened with work, I had no time to relish them, and the last five have brought me into another corner of the world to experience them with totally different feelings. But spring comes to all the world and when it comes it is all for all. It is strange how every aspect alters when spring is there: not only does it change the colour and form of material things, but also feeling and thought. A child, too young to walk, will sit in its pram, gazing round at the yellows, greens, and reds, and smile at a bird or kitten in the little garden. In boyhood, we want to rush away and tramp over the fields for a thousand miles, or cut off small flowering branches or catch birds, fly kites, sail boats, and play games on the green. In manhood, spring makes us wish for a lover, with whom we may walk together and admire the tiny crocus or primrose in soft tones, catching each other's gaze and letting our four eyes suddenly meet in one glance among the meadows. As soon as age comes along, the mind is less intense, and we shall walk slowly in the sunshine with laughter or a smile, thinking back over what we have done in the past at this time of the year; perhaps thinking we may not entertain many more springs, and so loving them more than before.

It is not easy for me to say the very day when spring comes to London or when it departs. London is always a little gloomy and chill, but when spring comes, though it is still very cold, the trees will burst into green in a few days. I must warn foreigners who have never been to London not to consider the green grass as a sign of spring there, because strange to say it is always green all the year round, a fact of which English people are reasonably proud. In China there is no green grass till spring comes.

Somewhere near the beginning of March, spring may come to London. Just on the eve of its coming one feels a little glow of warmth. Even before it shows any hint of arrival, I myself somehow feel it is on the way. This is not due to any occult art, but simply because I am often awakened by the clear and tender songs of the birds on the chestnut tree in front of my bedroom window. Of course, birds recognise spring first. We have all listened to a bird's song at some time, but the best time of all to enjoy it is while lying in bed in the very early morning. There is as yet no other sound, and one is still in a state of contentment and clouded thought just after a sound sleep. It is unpleasant to get up the moment one wakes, and what is better than to waste some time listening to the cheerful song of the birds? They sing with great beauty and in full throat at dawn before people are about, and they apparently never feel at ease singing after seven o'clock in the morning as one of our great dramatists has told us. It is true that we can rarely hear them sing with complete freedom in the day-time, unless we go into a forest. Birdsong enchants me, and I have grown into the habit of waking specially early to listen to it. I have often wished to be a musician so that I could compose those delicious notes into melodies. I once had the interesting experience of listening to a conversation between Mr. and Mrs. Nightingale at a performance of Bertram Mills's Circus at Olympia. Actually Mr. and Mrs. Nightingale were two handsome young gentlemen who tried to speak in bird language. All the audience was highly diverted, and there was nobody to find fault because they had no nightingale to sit in judgment.

After listening to the bird's song in bed, I sometimes spring up and hurry off to Hampstead Heath, which is not far from where I live. I can hear more there. This is a sort of game which we call in Chinese "Searching for spring," and we play it before any trees have shown a sign of the season. Although I have only done it a few times, I enjoyed myself immensely. Hampstead Heath is a place where I get all sorts of indications about the London seasons and I have no intention of leaving its neighbourhood as long as I am here. On the Heath the north wind might still be blowing chill to the bones, and trees standing in complete blackness as if it were mid-winter, but while I strolled about here and there and listened to the birds I would by chance suddenly find one or two very tiny yellow buds of crocuses or daffodils sticking out among the grass. Then I would jump up and say to myself, "I have found spring!" I once wrote a poem about "An early morning on Hampstead Heath," which runs:

Getting up in the early morning I listen to the song of the birds,
They chatter their happiness.
The distant trees gradually peer out of the mist,
A shadowy greenness obscuring the ground.
I love the birds' singing,
They make the landscape more graceful and charming.

In the busiest London streets one can hardly notice spring because all the buildings are packed so tightly beside each other, and the shopkeepers address their customers just as usual. They may mention a few words about the weather, such as "fine day" or "it gets warm now," but they do not hang the word "spring" on their lips unless you go to the tailor's. I often think that spring comes to Oxford Street and Piccadilly Circus first and to the rest of the streets in London afterwards, because the change in ladies' clothes makes a kind of weathercock. But the streets around the Royal Exchange and Gracechurch Street would be the last destinations for spring, as they are the haunts of men instead of fashionable ladies. Perhaps it will never go to Locksley Street or Pennyfields at all. Another sign of spring in Oxford Street is the window decoration of Selfridge's, and in Piccadilly Circus that of Swan and Edgar's. I feel one can easily tell the seasons in London if one just walks to and fro in front of Selfridge's windows.

But it is better to seek spring in the London parks, where the real tokens of spring are hung up on the top branches of the trees. Let me quote a few passages from an article which appeared in the *Observer*:

"Spring comes by fits and starts. Not many days ago we shivered in snow flurries carried on a biting north-easter. In the last few days we have rejoiced in a spring that has been very real and present. . . . It is the alternation of spring and lingering winter, sometimes swift and always vivid, that makes March a joy . . . with each passing day the sun strikes warmer, raising a thin steam from the damp earth and causing the primroses to shine more brightly. . . . The wheatear has been recorded and so has the yellow wagtail: and many plants no less than the birds are well in advance of their usual date. . . . Little rose-red buds, a tiny coral-like incrustation thickening the tangle of sombre twigs, adorn the blackthorn. The elms have reached that deep purple that precedes the green, and the most delicate of all greens is coming to the larches. . . . And already the birds sing with purpose—stormcock and throstle and blackbird, the while fieldfare and redwing do no more than dream of their northern homes. And from the budding hawthorn the chaffinch breaks from his eternal twink-twinking into full summer song. A few days ago it would have seemed impossible to lie comfortable and warm on an ivy bank with primroses and violets scenting the air, and with the quiet ripple of birds' song far and near. Now I have done so. . . ."

This describes in better words than I can find how the last traces of winter pass into early spring. A Chinese poet, Su Tung-P'o of Sung dynasty, once wrote a line "Spring water is warm in the stream—the wise ducks know it first." Another poet of a later period argued this point and said, "It is not even accurate; why, the geese know just as quickly as ducks about things like that—that man with his everlasting ducks . . .!"[1] Ah, Londoners would argue with the second poet as well and say: "Why not the sea-gulls or pigeons in the London parks?" It is all a matter of dispute, but I myself have a special affection for ducks, and in particular for those in St. James's Park. After many walks there by myself and with friends I shall always remember happily some of the scenes round the lake. In the early spring the weather was still very cold and there were only a few people wandering about. There I saw two or three ducks waddling down into the water from the little island, with its bare, black bushes in the morning mists, and floating towards me as if they knew I had food for them. As they floated down I noticed they would swing round in the middle of the lake, then swim back towards me, so that I should not think them too greedy and eager for my crumbs. If it was a windless day, the surface of the water would be so calm

[1] From *The Chinese Eye*, p. 124.

5

and flat that you could even count the ripples made by the ducks floating. If the weather was warm and the season full spring, there would be crowds of people sitting on the public chairs and walking along the water-side, and you would see a group of baby ducks beside the old ones. Probably they know how to float by instinct, and need only be careful to follow their mother. It is interesting to watch them minutely and see that they do not push or pull each other if they are left in a crowded group behind the mother, and how they play and talk together by beating their small beaks. They will swim along beside their mother to pick up the food, but if the mother duck suddenly lifts her head to float away, the youngsters will not stay eating, but lift their heads in turn to follow her away too. How closely they are attached to each other, mother and children! The baby ducks are even better behaved than some boys and girls. I have tried to paint them several times and written one poem about them in remembrance of a friend of mine:

The ducks in St. James's Park,
Float in groups on the green waves.
The trees all round are tossed in a mild breeze,
And my heart is encouraged to enjoy this lovely Nature.
The water is glass-clear down to the bottom,
Once it reflected the shadow of two passers-by, hand-in-hand.
But now my friend is far away.
Oh, ducks, ducks, how are you getting on?
I have too many thoughts, facing the wind.

Regent's Park is another place where I enjoy the springtime. The pigeons seem to flock there most of all. Sometimes an elderly man feeds them with peanuts; and sometimes a mother and her small girl. They light on your hands if you are not afraid of them, and they even take a rest on your head if you do not object. They are the friendliest birds. Once I saw a squirrel hurrying down from a big tree with his two eyes staring eagerly at me to see if I would give him something; as soon as he got the first bite he suddenly leapt on to a small branch of the tree and swung himself up and down with great joy. I made a painting of that afterwards. There are many huge swans in the Park which even have the daring to chase sailing-boats on the lake. Their long, upright necks are just like masts. One of my experiences of rowing there with my friends is recorded in this poem:

> *Wandering, talking and laughing the whole day,*
> *The waves turn green in the east wind of March.*
> *The skimming sound of the oars brings a delicate feeling;*
> *It is just like a dragonfly darting over the water.*

Increasing chatter in the parrot house and fiercer shaking of the railings and rattling and clattering in the monkey house are signs, too, that the animals in the Zoo are aware of spring coming. I love to watch the chimpanzees' tea-party, because I have never seen that sort of thing in my own country. While I write I call to mind the old male chimpanzee who died last year—how clever his tricks were! The seals are said to have a keen sense of music and I remember a holiday on the sea-coast of West Scotland, where seals came up in hordes on to the rocks of an island to which we had rowed and where we were playing the gramophone. As the pond in the Zoo is much too small, you would see them in early spring jumping in and out of the water as if they could never rest.

At Whipsnade Zoo the birds and animals get more space to play in. When I was there one spring I saw three or four peacocks walking around the bottom of a big tree, and one of them spread wide its huge tail like a painted screen with its head craning up towards the top of the tree. Then I noticed a macaw with deep-blue wings, red chest and long, red-and-gold tail standing there motionless. I wondered whether it knew that the peacock was staring furiously at it. They seemed to me very like two actresses quarelling behind the scenes after dressing up and before they went on to the stage. Fortunately I was not their producer, or I should have been in a fine pickle! The ostriches with their ridiculous long necks reminded me of the Guinness poster. But the polar bear was grumbling at such a hot London spring which kept him swimming about in the water hour after hour.

When spring has really come to London, I go to Kew Gardens to see the flowers—the crocuses, daffodils and primroses all over the ground, and the almond trees with their pink blossom shining out of a grey, misty background. I always mistake them for the blossoms of our winter-plum tree, which holds so honourable a place in Chinese literature and art. They have the similarity of blossoming before the leaves grow, but our plum blossom has scent and some varieties have a yellow colour, particularly delicate against the background of pure white snow. When we Chinese talk about the colour of pear blossoms, we generally say they are snow white. A Chinese dramatist, Li Li-Wen, said that he liked to look on this blossom better than to eat its fruit. He said: "The real snow is in the possession of Heaven, but this one belongs to the human world. The former lacks scent and the latter has both (scent and whiteness)." This is his reason. I myself like it because in Kew Gardens the pear trees are magnificently large and look like giants wearing robes all of white and standing with supreme dignity. The bright, aggressive, red colouring of rhododendrons must also attract people to these gardens: you cannot help being allured by them when they are in bloom. I myself like to rest my eyes from them by afterwards visiting the gentler-coloured lilacs.

When Easter has almost come, nearly every Londoner thinks of going away for his holidays. Every big station is crowded with holiday-makers. As I came from a country where no such term as Easter was heard until very recently, I was astonished at first to see so many merry-making people, and I wondered what was the meaning of it all. Later on, I began to appreciate it and am so used to it now that I make my own Easter excursion. Alas! how fast and deeply can environment change one's habits! From a friend of mine, I received my first Easter egg in London three years ago, and for a long time I could not stop looking at it and touching it. Naturally Londoners take Easter eggs for granted as it is their custom, but for a Chinese like me the Easter egg meant that I was in a foreign country. I consider London as my second home, still, a different custom will suddenly make me think of my birthplace.

I remember some one writing in *The Times* that the modern poet was not the first, and would not be the last, to feel that:

> *And since to look at things in bloom*
> *Fifty springs are little room.*

I find it very difficult to describe in detail what I have done during the past five springs. But there is one objectionable feature about them always in my mind, the tiresomely changeable weather. There might be one or two hot days but they rarely continue for a week. That journalist was very wise to give a sub-title "Hope of warmer days" when he described the severe Easter frost with snow, sleet, and hail showers. Although London spring has many attractions, Londoners who have not travelled much will hardly be able to imagine a Chinese spring, especially in *the South Country*, the part of South-east China along the southern side of the Yangtze River. It is the place I dream about when I meet spring in London. Once I wrote a poem while I was lying on Hampstead Heath:

> *Gradually accustomed to the habits of this sea-country,*
> *I rejoice in afternoon sleep on the meadow.*
> *The piled-up petals on the grass seem a foot deep of crimson*
> *   redness,*
> *After Spring comes, there is no dream not going to the south of*
> *   the Yangtze River.*

The third line can hardly describe the scenery of the Heath, but when I dream of *the South Country* of China, I can always see countless flowers and petals wherever I set my foot. There are numerous poems by our great masters describing the beauty of that part of my country. One wrote:

> *Rain fell on the trees in the South Country,*
> *Unnumbered flowers burst into bloom overnight.*

And another would persuade his friend to stay there and said "*If you catch up spring in the South Country, stay with her by all means.*" The following poem is frequently on all our lips:

> *So all the world praises the South Country to me:*
> *It best befits you a wanderer there to spend your life.*
> *The waters in Spring look bluer than the skies,*
> *And rains will lull you to sleep in the painted boat.*

10

PLATE I. *Morning mist in St. James's Park*

The wine-shop maids are as charming as the moon,
Their glowing arms like frozen frost and drifted snow.
Do not go home before you are old,
Lest you should break your heart.

Now I recall the joys of the South Country:
When I was young and my Spring attire was light,
On horseback I roamed by the arched bridge,
And on the terraces red sleeves beckoned at me;

Behind the emerald screen and the gold-knockered doors,
I got drunk and slept amid the thick-growing flowers of love.
Were I to see those flowers once again,
Even though my hair grew white, I swear, I would never come
home.[1]

Springtime in China is always warm, even if it is rainy. We have a very cold winter, much colder than in London, so we all long for spring the more. As soon as we know spring is on the way, we can look forward to warmer and warmer days. The longer spring stays, the warmer will be the weather. Every family gets to work packing away all their winter clothes and taking out spring ones. According to the old Chinese calendar we have a special day which we call "The Welcoming Spring" festival. All families prepare a sort of ceremony for it. It is said that the god of spring is a cowherd, and he will tramp around every house with his cow just to tell you he has come. I have never had the luck to meet him during my thirty springs in China, but at least was fortunate enough to get a fine dinner each time in celebration! After that we have a lantern festival which is also meant to celebrate the coming of spring. Again, on the twelfth day of the second moon,

---

[1] From Chinese Lyrics, translated by Ch'u Ta-Kao.

which will be in the middle of March on your calendar, a festival of flowers is held in certain parts of the country. Women and children prepare quantities of coloured paper streamers and silk favours of every tint and shade. On the appointed day they hang these on the flowers and flowering trees, reciting at the same time certain laudatory and congratulatory sentences, prostrating themselves. By this worship of flowers it is supposed that a fruitful season may be assured. These are only a few of our spring festivities.

God of Spring

What I have seen of people's reaction to spring in London is unlike our Chinese attitude. Perhaps our minds are curiously made. We not only try to enjoy ourselves in that season, but we express a certain emotion towards it. Perhaps you may say we are too sentimental! Not only do our scholars write poems to welcome spring, but they seem to keep the thought of spring in their minds constantly. They have written poems with such titles as: *Searching for Spring*, *Wandering about in Spring*, *Tramping in Spring*, *Asking about Spring*, *Trying to keep Spring*, *Pity for Spring's Going*, *Escorting Spring*, and many more. When we know spring is going, a group of people, men or women, will invite their friends to a gathering called "Bidding Farewell to Spring." They generally talk, write poems and paint pictures, and they will prepare a good dinner as well. We regret the passing away of spring more than most nations in the world, but spring is very cruel and stubborn and goes away at its own pleasure. It can never be persuaded. Heaven has set up the law that spring may come down to the world for a time and then must leave it. I really do not know why we should make so much complaint about its coming and going. Ah, the Chinese are very stupid! I would like to pay a compliment to Londoners; they are wise enough to walk about in the parks as usual and take very little notice of spring's departure.

Although I have had reason to enjoy my London spring, I have two unsatisfied desires. The first one you may smile at. I have a great longing to eat the food special to this season called "spring rolls." It is made of thin pastry wrapped round a few tender young leaves or buds of some special Chinese spring greens, with minced meat and mushrooms. It is quite possible to order this dish in one of the Chinese restaurants in London, but it can hardly compare with the native product. My second regret is that I have been unable to visit my ancestors' tombs these five years. Being brought up in the tradition of ancestor-worship, we generally visit our ancestors' temple and tombs once every year. It is always done in the spring season about Easter time. When this time comes, every family is busy making some preparation for it and the elders must take the younger members to visit the family tombs, so that thay shall learn to respect those who have benefited them, and love those whose kindness has brought them up. Every man who can get away from his job must try to be at home at that time. I never failed when I was in China. I used to visit the tombs of my parents more than once a year if I could. But now my home is too far away and I shall never be considered a filial son. Alas, this fault cannot be mended!

晨起聞鳥喧啾啾

鳴得意遠樹漸生

煙濛濛綠無地愛

爾群鳥聲風景添

幽媚　春日早起　曉

Translation of the poem is on page 3

Summer in London

In London a Chinese would say there is never any very hot weather and its hottest day is like the end of our spring. The clear division between spring and summer that we know in our country is unknown to Londoners. This simple observation brings me to thoughts of the contradictoriness of the world, and the arbitrary nature of all definitions.

For all that, Londoners mark out a day in the year when "summer-time" is to begin, though I am sure they would never know it without studying the daily papers. And yet this summer-time usually happens before Easter, and Easter is certainly associated with spring. How puzzling this London is to an Oriental mind!

I arrived in London on a June day in 1933 and it was raining. I felt chilly and thought it must soon be autumn. Later I was strolling by myself in Hyde Park for the first time, and suddenly I saw two ladies wandering about, and to my great surprise they wore fur coats! I knew it was summer and could not believe that the dreams of my younger days had come true. What dreams? There are many popular novels in China, describing people of divine power who are able to wear fur gowns in summer and very thin silk clothes in winter. If we ordinary people talked of wearing fur gowns in summer, we should feel our whole body being constricted and perspiration coming out from the roots of every hair, while the thought of silk clothes in winter would make us shiver. Most youngsters long to be divine, and after reading those novels in early boyhood I wished repeatedly to meet a demi-god like that. Now I have seen only too many of them. (I hope the ladies in London will be complimented.) I remember having used all the descriptive phrases from Chinese novels when I wrote to my nephews and nieces, telling them about the London *goddesses*, and they replied that I should not make London seem so exciting or they would be jealous and long to come too.

There are two plants which probably mark the real appearance of summer in London better than anything else, since heat and cold are small indication. I would choose the may tree first. There are a good number of them on Hampstead Heath, where I often go on summer mornings specially to look at them. Some are planted in a line where two small hills meet and they look like a pink-red wall in bloom. This tree in flower, with a few green leaves showing, delights me, and I particularly like to look at the arrangement of the branches with their curious shapes, for they add to my knowledge of tree painting. The second plant is the bluebell. I was persuaded by my landlady to go and see them in Kew Gardens for the first time. We went there together while I was still a stranger to the gardens, and she had not been there for many years. We wandered in many directions before we found the blue-bell walk. Talking and walking here and there very slowly, in the distance I suddenly saw a big strip of bright blue on the ground under a cluster of dark greens; in between the sun was shining. As soon as we reached it, I knew that never in my life had I seen such a mass of bright-blue colour together. It is impossible for any human being to attempt to imitate a colour which has been displayed by nature so evenly and refreshingly. My companion was very interested in Queen Victoria's cottage, which some artist sitting on the path was sketching, and

I stood there too to let my eyes watch the movement of the shadow of the clouds on the bluebells made by the veering sunbeams. The differences of the colours reflected on the bluebells were indescribable!

The next time I went to the bluebell walk was after the death of this same landlady, a short time ago. But all the flowers were faded. I wrote a poem afterwards on Queen Victoria's cottage:

Built in Kew Gardens for the peaceful evening time,
From the bluebells overblown comes a lingering fragrance,
I visit the relics of a hundred years past,
The small cottage is lonely against the setting sun.

Nature remains changeless, but the human part in her seldom stays unaltered. Within five short years I have faced many changes of friends, and those who have died are always in my memory—my kind landlady, companion of the bluebells, not excepted. I like to listen to the song of the cuckoo in Kew Gardens, but it can only be heard by chance, because I think they are not familiar haunters of the place. There is a legendary story attached to this bird which has great significance for our farmers and poets. It is said that the ancestors of this bird were fed in the heavenly palace, being the favourites of the Western Queen Mother who lived in Heaven. Once they misbehaved themselves, so the Western Queen Mother punished them and ordered them to bring their young down once every year (generally at the beginning of May) in order to urge our farmers to hasten with their cultivation of the rice-fields. Naturally those who have lived in Heaven do not care to come down to live in the human world, so the cuckoo's song is really a gloomy and melancholy cry. Its sound has been interpreted in the Chinese language in

PLATE II. *Summer afternoon in Kew Gardens*

many ways; according to one of them it means "Hurry-up, hurry-up, start the crop"; as soon as our farmers hear it, they ought to get busy in the field, cultivating, sowing, weeding, watering, etc. These birds are not allowed to return to Heaven again until the rice and wheat are nearly ripe. By that time the cuckoos have no more tears left to shed from their eyes, but only blood. And these blood-tears drop down on the hedges of the fields all over the country-side, and become flowers which we call "cuckoo-flowers," funnel-shaped and of blood-red colour on low bushes. In May and June most of our country-side is covered with this kind of flower. Our poets, if they are away from home at that season and hear the cuckoo crying, immediately begin to think of country labours and long to be back to take part in them. If they tried hard to get back but in vain, they would describe their tears as "red as cuckoo-flowers." This expression occurs over and over again in the verses of our great masters. I remember an English poem on a cuckoo by E. R. A. in the *Observer*, based on a less romantic and melancholy idea. If I quote it in contrast, you may realise the difference between Eastern and Western mentality:

St. Peter, Minor, sits in state,
The guardian of the Golden Gate
Beyond the chilly stairs that climb
To roses and the Summer-time.

He sits and snoozes in his chair
(It must be dreary, waiting there),
Unheeding though the birds salute
The day with psaltery and flute.

The wheels of the returning year
Awake him not, nor does he hear

The pipes of Pan upon the hill,
The trumpet of the daffodil.

The robin taps: he does not stir:
The linnet gives a timid "Sir!"
The North Wind batters at the door,
And gets no answer but a snore.

And then there comes a double knock,
Sharp and peremptory: at the shock
The Saint starts up, takes from his side
The key, and throws the portal wide.

I have written several poems about Kew Gardens and would like to quote two more here in order to show my mood there on two different occasions. The following one I wrote when I went there just after summer came and my attention was caught by a crane:

Who has sent the cuckoo's call to lead away the last days of spring?
Dense green has just regarlanded the willow bank.
An old crane flies down with a wild motion
And stands alone at the stream head fearless of man.

But the other one was written when I went there on a very fine summer day and was absorbed in the water-lilies and geese:

There are geese and water-lilies in Kew Gardens,
The petals of the lilies and the shadow of the geese are
always mingling.
How full the goose's feather,
And the petal is not without charm!
Floating among the lilies in the morning,
Resting in the midst of them at evening,

Sometimes they lift their necks with yearning call,
While the lilies seem elated and flush deeper rose.
If the lilies are battered by wind and rain
The geese will cry in low voice with shrunken neck.
The love world knows no difference between man and Nature,
I envy both of you in your happy companionship.

It was a very hot day when I wrote this and the sun shone brightly. Although the heat was nothing compared with what we have in China in summer, it was warm enough to make one feel sleepy. I carefully watched four or five geese come up from the water and stand by the side of the pond. Soon they all fell asleep. One stood on one foot, the others hid their heads under their wings, or among their back feathers. There was only one with eyes half-open, letting its eyelids drop slowly from time to time, which tempted me also to drowsiness. Afterwards I tried to make a picture of it. (Plate II.)

Cicada on the willow branch

In China, we are not only driven to sleep by the oppressive heat, but we always feel drowsy when we hear the disturbing sound of the cicada. This insect is a great feature of the Chinese summer. Its sound is somewhat like that of machines continuously moving in a factory, but a little softer than most. It starts on a very low and slow note, and then gradually reaches a high-pitched whirling sound as if so hard pressed by the heat that it can only scream. The cicadas generally perch up on the top branches of willows or other leafy trees. At the time of great heat most people keep in a cool place inside their houses, and the only sound they can hear outside is not that of cars or any sort of traffic but the cicada, which always reminds people how hot it is, and sends them to sleep.

Another feature of the Chinese summer is the lotus flower. Westerners will have some idea of its appearance from the decorations of Chinese vases or from most specimens of Chinese porcelain or painting. We like it especially because of its big, clear-scented flower on a long, thin stem coming out well above the water, and its huge, umbrella-like leaves. The lotus symbolises "purity" because it rises so pure and with such clear scent out from the muddy bottom of the lake or pond. It also grows fruit, and the centre of the fruit, which is not like a stone, can be dried and mixed with tea leaves for making tea. Sometimes we keep a handful of tea leaves in the bud of the lotus flower for a day or two in order to absorb the scent; then the tea produces a delicate and subtle flavour. Again, some of our tea-experts have the custom of collecting dewdrops from the lotus leaves every morning and making tea with them. Though I have seen some lotus flowers in Kew Gardens, they were kept in a hot-house even in summertime. The London summer is too chilly for them.

I consider the weather of London in summer-time partly like our spring and partly our autumn. We like these two seasons very much, so I always write to my fellow-countrymen and advise them to come to London in summer if they have enough money to travel. Every year at the end of June and the beginning of July here people are talking about their holiday preparations, and the stations are packed with even more people, with their cases and luggage, than at Easter time. I am sure London is much emptier in summer. There are fewer and fewer people walking in the streets. Therefore I come out of my shell much more than usual. In springtime I like to walk in the London parks, but in summer I like to walk on the roads. Exhibition Road is one of my favourites, because it is very wide and gives me the sensation of being able to expand. Also it is very long, which allows my eyes to see things in a far distance. While walking there I have never felt crushed and cramped. The next road I like to walk in is Cromwell Road. Although there may be more cars there, yet it is wide enough for me to take no notice of them. Besides there are many big buildings with good architectural design, and these give an added feeling of comfort. I also like to walk along Hall Road and Holland Park Road around St. John's Wood area. As I have been living in Hampstead for more than four years, the longest road in London, Finchley Road, has known my steps on very many occasions. I like to walk there on summer mornings because the thin mist continually hides its ending from my eyes. By the way, though Londoners like to get away for holidays in summer-time, yet I find many more foreigners coming in to take their place. I have the same experience about week-ends too, because most Londoners can get away, but foreigners can only remain to walk along the streets.

We could never imagine that a fire would be necessary in summer-time, but my experience in London has taught me differently. Most families have a fire the whole year round. I remember I had on one occasion asked a few friends to sit by the fire for a chat in the middle of August and then I wrote a poem:

> *Summer rain produces a strange coldness,*
> *Hugging the fire my friends make idle gossip.*
> *I speak of many treasures from the East,*
> *They hear me, with regret for time's passing.*
> *Chatting goes on even after the rain stops,*
> *Never did I know greater happiness in my life.*

23

On another occasion I met with one of the biggest hail showers I have known. It was during summer in London about four years ago. A Swiss friend of mine asked me to take her to Lyndhurst Road off Haverstock Hill. It was a very sunny day and we walked up from one end of Parkhill Road. A few hundred yards up from Belsize Park tube station, it began raining, but we both knew what London rain would be like, so we just walked on. Soon I felt my head being hit by small particles. Before we realised it everybody was running and scattering in a very disorderly manner to escape this tremendous shower of hail. It seemed to me that Heaven was pouring down a stream of cube-sugar! We took shelter in a public bar. There were too many people there and some of them were completely drunk. But it was hardly possible to move and there were even no cars running, and the roads were full of water. For nearly an hour traffic was stopped. How strange the weather of London is!

In London fur coats and fires persist month after month, and so do the identical vegetables and fruits, and this benefit of science, I find, makes life monotonous. When I think of the different seasons in my country I generally cannot prevent myself from mentioning the seasonable fruits and vegetables. In summer we have a great variety of melons either for eating or for cooking, which produce different flavours. One of them which I particularly like is called "fragrant" melon, and I eat it by itself—its flavour and natural coolness are just like a very good ice-cream. And the other, which is called "silky" melon, is in the form of a thick cord; when it is cooked to make a clear soup it is most refreshing. Besides we have different kinds of pears, and also water caltrops, lotus stem, and so on. It is a great joy to follow girls rowing on the lakes and picking them or to listen to the girls singing the song of picking water caltrops or lotus seeds, while a breeze blows over the surface of the water under a colourful sunset. Alas, how much I long to do that again!

An American friend of mine told me one day that English people think America has nothing but holidays. Perhaps Londoners will think we have even more than Americans, if I confess we have many summer festivals as well as the spring ones I mentioned before. But we have not had the "week-end" habit, except in a few big towns, until recently. I will only describe one of these summer festivals here, though to be accurate the Chinese poets arbitrarily dubbed it an autumn one. It is held on the seventh night of the seventh moon (about the end of August) and celebrates a very ancient love-story. It is said that a certain weaving-girl, the grand-daughter of the Emperor of Heaven, lived east of the "Silver River," which is our Chinese name for the Milky Way. She toiled year after year weaving the "cloud-embroidered, heavenly dress." The Emperor of Heaven, seeing that she was diligent and lonely, had pity on her and married her to a herd-boy who lived west of the Silver River. Unfortunately after she was married she became less diligent in the Emperor's service and gave up her weaving. The Emperor became angry and made her for punishment return to her old home on the east of the river. Only once a year, on the seventh night of the seventh moon, was she allowed to go and see her herd-boy at the west of the river. Every year when the night came, it is said that all the blackbirds in Heaven would of their own accord gather together and form a bridge over the Silver River, across which the weaving-girl could walk to meet the herd-boy. And on the same night, on earth, girls hold parties, invite their friends to offer sacrifice to the weaving-girl and pray her to grant them skill in weaving and needlework, and especially a good future husband—hence the "Festival of Wishing for Skill." I think myself that the Emperor of Heaven did some injustice to the herd-boy! Ch'in Kuan of Sung dynasty wrote a famous poem about it:

(Herd-boy):

The soft clouds make decorations,
The shooting stars play harbinger—
Far across the Silver River you secretly come to me,
Though only once a year we meet in the time of sharp wind
*   and chill dew,*
We are many times happier than the lovers on earth.

(Weaving-girl):

Our feelings are tender as water,
Our meeting is sweeter than a dream;
It is hard for me to look back on the homeward path from the
*   Blackbirds' Bridge.*
But if our love for each other will endure,
It makes no difference that we do not live together day and
*   night.*[1]

The last two lines have won the heart of every one of us who has been in love, ever since. But it is said one night's time in Heaven is far longer than one in the human world. So that makes a difference!

[1] Translated by Ch'u Ta-Kao.

出園初夏

Translation of the poem is in the middle of page 20

Autumn in London

Is there any autumn in London? You may say there is, but it is hardly autumn in our sense. The cicada, which I mentioned in the last chapter, tells us in China when autumn is coming—its cry gradually becomes fainter and shorter, uttered at intervals instead of continuously. It is no longer compelled to scream from heat and is content with the cool air, so that it does not want to cry any more, as most of our poets describe it doing. I daresay it is easy to imagine how much joy we derive from the air growing cooler and cooler after a continuous and exhausting heat which made us unwilling to move. This cooler air is so fresh and clear and cloudless that it persuades us to think the sky is much higher than usual. If we feel like that we have a feeling of freedom and expansion inside our bodies as well. Thin clothes and tasty foods are all at our disposal at this season. When we are amusing ourselves or watering our gardens, we may suddenly hear one or two cries of the wild geese from a very remote distance in the sky and then we can see a group of them flying high up in orderly formation which we interpret as one or two simple Chinese characters. It is said in China that these wild geese generally come at this time every year when the air becomes cooler, while the swallows go to a warmer land instead. The swallows will come again in spring and the geese go back to their old place. This exchange suggests plenty of different moods to our poets and also makes it easy for us to realise the seasons. But, after all, what is there to tell me that autumn has come to London?

In the city and in the streets there is no sign of autumn at all, unless perhaps one can again get some sort of information from Selfridge's window!

There is a surer sign by which I could know autumn here, that is the railway stations. From the middle of September I can see people crowded there again, coming back from their holidays. Their faces show a change in colour which makes me think of the changed colour of the tree leaves. They seem to have come back to tell me that autumn is here, but I usually want to ask them why they come back just now—in autumn-time, because we always choose this period of the year to go away, especially to travel to mountains and on rivers.

Autumn colours may be decorating the trees along London roads, yet those yellowish greens and reds are often covered with thick mist or fog and too obscured to be noticeable. And as the trees along the road are not very big, these colours hardly stand out against the buildings, so they are always ignored. London is always in a hazy atmosphere, or as most Londoners call it "honeyish colour." The colours of autumn on the trees change very quickly and the leaves fall down as fast as we can watch them. Therefore, autumn in London is very short!

Practically speaking, autumn is not to be found in London town itself, but more in the parks and around the suburbs. The places in which I like to walk during this time are the open fields of Golder's Green, Edgware, Wormwood Scrubs, and Wimbledon Common. Even more attractive to me and easy to reach is Ken Wood on Hampstead Heath. Although I go there about twice a week, I like to be there in autumn better than at any other time. It is hard to tell the reason why, but I just feel so, as if I could detect the slight difference between the singing of birds in spring and autumn there. One morning last autumn my breath was suddenly taken away by a dense red layer on the treetops (behind the building) when I came over the small bridge crossing the pond. Below the red layer was the dark mass of the trees and then came the wide fresh meadow. On the meadow only a few red leaves had fallen and were lying there, telling me that autumn was in full swing and that the leaves were just turning red. The autumn wind was chilly, but the air fresh. Except for a young lady sitting on the seat under an elm tree, I was the only person in sight. The swans were more lively than usual on that particular morning and I guessed they felt the gusty winter was on the way and they had to be more active to reserve some heat for it. Somehow I have a queer idea that I like to look at the white feathers of the swan reflected under a mass of red leaves better than under a mass of green. The following poem was written on that occasion:

> *The Ken Wood trees are as red as fire,*
> *Stretched beneath—a green plain.*
> *The pine wind soughs mildly,*
> *Its cool feeling touches and its coolness lingers in my*
> *   garments.*
> *A young girl in quiet retirement*
> *Sits alone reading her lover's letter.*
> *The white swans do not understand this;*
> *Sometimes they glide up to the trees and pry at her.*

I think there is another place to see real autumn in London, that is Epping Forest. During these five years I have been there more than a dozen times. Whether I go with friends or by myself, I always like to be there about September. It is such a huge place that I cannot say even now where I have been and where not. I never bothered to remember the names of places, but just strolled about

PLATE III. *Early Autumn in Ken Wood*

here and there without thinking of the way back; sometimes it took me more than an hour to walk to the bus-stop. Once I went there with three friends who were all good walkers. We talked and walked a long way until we reached the pool, where there were a great many rowing-boats. My eyes leapt across the pool to the other side with keen interest as I did not know what might lie behind the dark woods. I persuaded them all to go in that direction. As we went along the ground was very muddy, but full of a fresh smell of undergrowth, and I could see a few leaves already turned yellow standing out in the bright sunshine. My friends were good talkers too; they seemed to have plenty to say and just went on talking without noticing where they were going. Fortunately they took no notice of me at all, sometimes I just interjected one or two words and sometimes I was left behind in complete silence to occupy my eyes with objects that pleased me. I teased them by saying that they had entirely achieved the English manner of walking! When I was a child in China, I heard from my grandfather that English people had long, straight legs without knees, though I knew from his manner that he was joking. But I almost believed it after being here for some time, and I should not only say that English people have straight legs, but they have very long necks, too! When I have seen them walking in the parks or any of the quieter roads, they just stretch out their long necks and straight legs and stride on and on with eyes staring straight ahead. If they have companions they may link their arms together and keep in step, but even if they talk they do not turn their faces to each other. This kind of motion can be well understood if one watches the step of the Guards in front of St. James's Palace. After I explained this, my friends just laughed and seemed to be proud of their achievement and went on again in a more exaggerated manner than before. Afterwards I was struck by a very beautifully shaped pine tree on the way and stood there to study it for quite a long time. When I realised that my friends had gone out of sight, I had to quicken my steps to find them. As soon as I caught sight of them on the top of a small hill, I could see they were sitting down and talking still; from a distance they were clearly enjoying the sunset. It was a very fine evening and the sunset looked much more ravishing than any I had ever seen in town. I had seen it on Hampstead Heath, as well as in Hyde Park where I looked at it through the boughs against the background of Bayswater Road, but it could never be better than here. In front of us, there were very thick woods covered with the rising evening mists, and when I looked far away I thought the mists were in thin layers one after the other as if they were hill ranges. The upper layer of the mist was very thin and of a greyish-green colour which turned into purple when it met the edge of the sunset. The colour of the sunset kept changing as we sat there. At first the sun looked bigger and nearer to us and then it was hidden behind blazing clouds. At the edge of the lower clouds shone out a very brilliant golden colour, and not only in one place: all about the circumference of the sun, the sky shone in many tones of gold, hardly to be described by pen; the nearer the brighter. After some time, the golden colour gradually changed into yellowish red and then reddish purple. Then it converged into a sharp-red mass in the middle with a thin, bluish-purple layer covering the outer parts. It made the whole surrounding seem tinged with a red glow. Although the tree leaves were all green except some that had turned a pale yellow, they were transformed into a colour neither green nor red, and the faces of my friends themselves turned reddish yellow. I profoundly enjoyed the scene. Afterwards the evening

wind blew us along with a chilly feeling on the way home.
I wrote a poem there too:

> *Where the opal mist rises is like piled up ranges of hills.*
> *We sit together deep in the woods to watch dusk fall.*
> *I only fear the evening beams prepare to fade. . . .*
> *The wind on a thousand firs chills us with rainy sound.*

When I went there again one autumn day entirely by
myself, I came to an astonishing place where there were
huge tall trees with very big trunks. Nearly all the leaves
had turned yellow, red, and brown, and the whole ground
was thickly covered with them. When I lifted my head, I
could only look at the sky in small white spots through
the leaves as most of the branches crossed each other, and
I really did not know how high the sky was. Everything
around me was yellow, red, and brown, even the trunks of
the trees had somewhat that effect. It seemed to me that
I was in an old Imperial palace at Peiping or a big
monastery at Hangchow in my country, which had many
big, dark-red, wooden pillars in the grand hall and the
walls decorated with yellow and red leaves. While I was
walking amidst the trees, I felt myself so little and infini-
tesimal and could only hear the sound of my own feet
tramping on the fallen leaves. I learned afterwards it was
raining outside, but I did not know it then. Yet I was
imagining a painting of a very tiny figure walking in between huge trunks of trees in rain with nothing but red
leaves on the ground. It would be really a lovely one!
Here is another poem of mine to describe it:

> *Epping Forest's beautiful colouring*
> *Reaches perfection as Autumn comes.*
> *It sheds a queer shadow on the Eastern stranger*
> *Walking slowly in the woods and trampling on red leaves.*

The red leaf, I could never describe better than did the English poet, Coleridge, in his lines:

> *There is not wind enough to twirl*
> *The one red leaf, the last of its clan,*
> *That dances as often as dance it can.*
> *Hanging so light, and hanging so high,*
> *On the topmost twig that looks up at the sky.*

But I would like to mention here an ancient Chinese love-story concerning those red leaves. In T'ang dynasty, there were thousands of young, intelligent girls kept in the Imperial palaces, but most of them just lived there at ease and died without even a single glance from the Emperor. They had beautiful houses to live in, delicious foods to eat and charming clothes to wear; but they lacked one thing which could never be bought or enticed by money or any material thing and which was so deeply rooted in the individual heart—that was the word "Love." When we refer to this word, our poets generally depict the sorrow of those ladies in the palaces. It was said that a Lady Han in the Imperial palace of T'ang Emperor Hsuan Tsung once wrote a poem on a big red leaf and let it float to the outside of the Imperial palace down a stream in the Imperial garden. The poem was as follows:

> *How swiftly does the flowing water tumble?*
> *Deep in the palace idleness all day long*
> *From my heart I thank the red leaf—*
> *Go carefully now into the world of men!*[1]

There are many stories about this poem. One of them states that after a long time the leaf was picked up by a

---

[1] Translated by Miss Innes Jackson.

soldier on guard outside the Imperial city. Though he did not realise the significance of the poem, yet he thought it must be an important thing belonging to the palace, so he reported it to his superior officer. As soon as this reached the ears of the Emperor, he ordered a search to be made among the court ladies. Naturally the Lady Han could not escape discovery. She imagined a heavy punishment would be put upon her, but on the contrary she was given in marriage to the soldier by Imperial order, which was an honourable thing. We just think how happy they both must have been at that time, even though the soldier might only earn a few pieces of silver a month. The Westerner might think that since they had never known each other it would be very difficult for them to live happily, but we believe that "Love" has a divine power which can bind two entirely different factors together if it has already been so arranged in heaven. Lady Han had this belief, so she let the red leaf float out to him to whom she was bound by this divine power. So although the red leaf is a symbol of autumn, it also has another meaning in our hearts.

Though autumn in London always slips by without my notice, yet if I see the date in the calendar, I cannot help thinking of the great "mid-autumn" festival we would be having in China. It is held on the fifteenth day of the eighth moon (about the middle of September or a little later). On this particular date every wanderer from his native home must try to get back, or if this is impossible, his or her heart is sure to be there, because we consider this a day of reunion and it is now that the moon reaches her perfection and is brighter and fuller than at any other time. But our lovers, brothers, or sisters, if they are separated or cannot see each other, would be full of thought and would generally write to express their feelings in poetry on this night. Su Tung-P'o of Sung dynasty wrote the following example while he was drinking on a mid-autumn night and thinking of his young brother:

When did the moon begin to shine?
Lifting my cup I ask of Heaven.
I wonder in the heavenly palaces and castles
What season it is tonight.
I wish to go up there on the wind,
But am afraid the crystal domes and jade halls would be too
 cold on high.
So I dance with my limpid shadow
As if I were no longer on earth.

Around rich bowers,
Into sweet boudoirs,
Shining upon the inmates still awake,
The moon should have no regrets.
Why is she always at the full when men are separated?
Men have their woe and joy, parting and meeting;
The moon has her dimness and brightness, waxing and waning.
Never from of old has been lasting perfection.
I only wish that you and I may be ever well and hale,
That both of us may watch the fair moon, even a thousand
 miles apart.[1]

Since I have been in London I have never failed to exchange thoughts in poetry with my only beloved elder brother on this occasion each of the past five years. He generally wrote me a very long poem but my reply was only a short one, usually about four lines. I do not think it is good to try and force out poetry, because it cannot be achieved by effort if the mood is lacking. To my sorrow, not very long ago I heard of his sudden death from a heart

[1] Translated by Ch'u Ta-Kao.

37

attack, and while I write now there is great and deep grief in my heart, all my thoughts pour into my head and tears fall down in streams from my eyes, preventing me from writing more!

Now let me tell you some more about this festival. It is supposed to be the birthday of the moon. At this time all the sweet-shops produce a great variety of seasonable cakes, which we call "Moon-Cake," and those especially which are made in Canton in South China are very famous. We generally have a specially good dinner on all festival days, and this certainly is no exception. After the dinner every family performs a ceremony in honour of the moon as she comes up into the middle of the sky. We generally put a square table in our courtyard or garden where the moon can directly shine on it. On the table all sorts of sweets and fruits are arranged in beautiful order and in the middle is set a huge, round moon-cake. After burning incense and letting off fireworks, father and mother will tell their children not to go near the table, because the moon is going to come down to eat the cakes. So they stand upright and hold their breath in a corner of the courtyard or under a tree of the garden to watch the moon. About twenty years ago I remember a very young cousin of mine being rather impatient and asking my grandmother after she had watched for sometime: "Why does the moon come down so slowly and how can she eat all the cakes, as every family is giving her some?" "Of course," grandmother answered, "She cannot eat them all. She is just coming down to touch the cakes a little in every house. After she has been, then you can have the cakes to eat." My little cousin was delighted to hear that!

The most popular and famous food in our autumn is crabs, but they are not like your sea-crabs which taste like lobsters; ours come from fresh water, as we have so many lakes. We can have them from the end of September until the beginning of December. At this time their flesh and oils have reached their tastiest and they are never caught at any other time. They are twice or three times as small as yours, but they are perfect in colour, taste, and flavour. There are many ways of cooking them, but one of the best

Moon, Chrysanthemum, wine, and crab

is just to steam them for a certain time. Then we open the shell and take out the flesh with its own oil, dipping it into the soya sauce and a special vinegar of Cheng-chiang with small pieces of ginger-roots in it. This gives an indescribable taste with which no other can compare. Li Li-Wen, the great dramatist whom I have mentioned before, has written a book on food in which he says he can describe the beauty and flavour of any food except crabs. He was always longing for them and never stopped eating them from the first day of their season until its end. There is an art in eating them as well. Most of our food experts,

39

especially ladies, can eat the flesh and oil after opening the shell and then put the shell together again like an uneaten one. Although I have eaten crabs all the autumn days of every year while I was in China, yet I never achieved this art. My grandmother used to scold me for having wasted too much even when I was grown up.

Besides crabs we have another symbol of autumn, that is the chrysanthemum flower. We love this flower for its great variety in colour and form, and furthermore we love it because it can blossom through the bitter autumn wind and heavy frost, symbolising a very strong character. There are many chrysanthemums in London about the same time too, but I am afraid I must say that they are rather limited in colour and shape. It is a strange coincidence that the leaves of chrysanthemums can be used for wiping fingers after eating the crabs, to take away the smell. Crabs, chrysanthemums, wine, and the moon are the four joys of our scholars, poets, and artists; they have been admired in numberless works. It is sheer joy to take a few steamed crabs, with a bottle of wine, and sit and eat them among chrysanthemums, occasionally looking up to watch the rising of the moon! Perhaps most of the busy common people neglect the moon and chrysanthemums, but they never forget crabs and wine. One crab costs very little in our money. I would go back to my own country merely to eat the crabs again!

海邦風味漸能語
綠地遽然午睡酣
艸上落花紅一尺
春來無夢不江南

小睡

[illegible]

Translation of the poem is on page 10

Winter in London

Winter in London makes everybody shiver. Without having been in London one is pretty sure to have heard tales of London's weather, and particularly about its winter habits. There are two lines of a poem written by our great poet, Su Tung-P'o of Sung dynasty about the weather of an island called Hai-Nan in the south of China, which say: "*All four seasons are Summer, one fall of rain and Autumn comes.*" I have made another two lines in the same manner for London: "*A few sunny days make one feel Spring, but there is no time with Winter away.*" I daresay some people may be indignant with me, but I suspect I am right!

It seems to me that men can live in London without paying heavy tailors' bills! Two or three suits will be plenty for a good long time unless one is extravagant or a dandy. It is a different story in China where we are obliged to have at least four different gowns for each season. It is also interesting for me to notice that the colour of most Londoners' clothes is very dark—either navy blue, brown, or black—as if the dullness of the weather influences them. I daresay society young men go in for bright colours, but I certainly have never come across them.

A Chinese lady told me once that she could not tell, on seeing an English lady in the street, whether she belonged to the Royal Family or was only a shopgirl, because all women wore dresses of more or less the same style and colour. The quality of the materials may be slightly different, but to a foreigner this is not apparent. I then said: "That comes from English democracy." But perhaps

42

PLATE IVa. *Snow on Hampstead Heath*
PLATE IVb. *Coalman in Rain*

democracy is helped by nature, because London's weather prevents any further variety.

I was often told that John Bull seldom went out without an umbrella, or its substitute, a stick, if it was fine. I do not see many Londoners carrying sticks in the street, but an umbrella they seem to have all the time. Whenever I see a person walking in the street with an umbrella I shall certainly say he is a typical Londoner, cautious and sensitive to the weather. It seems that the umbrella habit is rooted in the English mind at an early stage, because I never see a Westminster schoolboy going out without an umbrella besides his top-hat and huge collar. Every lady carries one too. I always take count of it as a part of the decoration attached to her dress. As this is such an important item and English people have a high reputation for carefulness, I can hardly believe that there are always a lot of umbrellas in the Lost Property Office in Baker Street! In China we need not carry an umbrella with us unless it is raining before we start out, as we generally can tell the weather for the day in the morning. I myself had no such friendship with umbrellas in the past, so I have never been persuaded into buying one for myself since I have been here. Luckily London rain has very seldom been pouring down in such a torrent as to soak through my clothes!

I have read a very interesting passage in one of our ancient classics *Tso Chuan*, which was written about the fifth century B.C. It gives a strange idea about weather, as follows:

"Another Marquis of Chin fell ill and the Earl of Ch'in sent Doctor Ho to attend the Marquis. After examining the case the doctor said: 'Your disease is incurable. It is neither caused by demons nor by food. You are under the spell of female charms which is poisonous like *Ku* (in Chinese). The good minister will die and heaven will not protect him.' The Marquis inquired: 'Are women not to be approached?' Ho answered: 'Only in strict moderation. There are six kinds of weather which give birth to the five tastes, the five colours, and the five sounds. When in excess each causes disease. The six kinds of weather are cloudy, clear, windy, rainy, misty, and bright. They form the four seasons and follow the order of the five elements. If the balance is disturbed dire consequences will result. Excessive cloudiness causes cold diseases, excessive clearness causes hot diseases, excessive wind causes painful limbs, excessive rain causes bowel complaints, excessive mist causes sensuality, and excessive brightness causes heart troubles. Now women are related to cloudiness and mist. Excessive contact with them produces internal heat ending in *Ku* disease. . . .' "[1]

A few terms in this passage have no bearing on what I am writing, yet it seems to me that our ancient genius had already in those days foretold London weather and its consequences. Surely excessive cloudiness, excessive wind, and excessive rain must be the reason why every Londoner has to have a doctor in constant attendance. We Chinese do not have a doctor attached to everyone and we do not go to doctors unless we are really ill. As for excessive mist, it makes me understand why Londoners are so fond of Scottish ales and Irish stout!

But London's weather is a help in one way—there is nothing more interesting than to talk about it! Two people who do not know each other, and do not particularly want to become acquainted, can sit on the public seats in parks or in the same railway compartment and talk about

[1] Translated by Dr. Wang Chi-I.

the weather for hours on end. If, in any gathering, conversation begins to lag, one can easily fall back on this interesting topic with a congenial companion. I always admire this kind of talk, and it seems to me that Londoners are of a friendly nature and live in a weather brotherhood without any necessity of knowing each other intimately. I had often heard that the English manner is very cool, like their weather, but I think that is not so when they talk about it. I especially admire the choice of wording in their weather forecast, such as—"The weather will be *mainly* fair, *moderate*, *little change*, or *unsettled with rain at times*," and so forth. All these expressions explain London's weather well. They never give a definite idea of what is going to come, but you are certainly sure about it in your mind—it will be a case of bringing umbrellas with you always!

In winter I have often been asked how I liked the weather in London if I was meeting someone for the first time. While I was hesitating how to answer, the questioner, if a man, would screw up his nose and say: "Oh, you don't like it, I suppose." If it was a lady, she would shrug her shoulders and just say "Horrible!" Of course they knew what I would answer and thought they had better say it for me. But though people know beforehand what the reply will be, yet they still like to ask this question. After a time, I learnt a good answer for it: "I am used to it now," to which the questioner can only say "Oh!" A Chinese lady once wrote to me from Germany: "English people are the most understanding and sensitive persons in the world! (I hope she is not imitating most English people who say anything English is always the best in the world!) When you meet them for the first time or even if you have known them for some time, they will never ask you about your private affairs. It is not as here (in

46

Germany) or in Italy or some other places in Europe, where the people are so keen to know other people's affairs, asking me such questions as 'how much money I have, whether I am married or not, what kind of business I am doing, how much my salary is.' These questions make me embarrassed and bored. But English people are always very polite and only ask about the weather. . . ." Although I have not actually stayed in any other country yet, I am beginning to wonder whether this is really the reason why the English like to talk about the weather.

In spite of all I have said about London weather, especially in winter-time, yet I like it in some ways. When winter is really in London, the leaves of the trees have all fallen and the whole body of branches and trunks is deep black. When those trees expose themselves entirely naked before the eye, showing the way of arrangement of the branches and their interlacing of each other, I find more beauty in them than I can easily describe. It is a sight that I never get tired of looking at and I love to make studies of them continually. Most European painters employ models for their work, but I feel somehow that the models are not so natural as they should be because their movements are dictated by the artist. I have often heard that some great masters used to employ a group of models and let them walk about freely in the studio. If they once saw a movement which was striking, then they would ask the model to pose in that position for them. This is a very good method. But I am afraid that most of the poorer artists nowadays cannot afford to have such a big studio and employ a whole group of models. I think I prefer to look at the trees—to look at the naked trees of which there are so many in London, and all to be seen without any payment. (I hope the Chancellor of the Exchequer will not impose a rate on them for the next budget after he knows that I am taking this advantage!) And I also like the unique colour which London's winter has lent to houses, church towers, trees, and railings amid their grey and white shroud of vapour. One day a fellow artist of my country came to see me. I learned that he had been trained in painting in the Western manner and had just arrived in London. Unfortunately it was winter-time. I thought he must have continually been out painting ever since he arrived. But to my surprise he said: "There is nothing worth painting in London now. When you go out, you can only see the moving heads of people, tobacconists, and sweet-shops. All the buildings are grey or dark in colour, and the trees are dead black. There is really not a single thing that could be painted here." As he uttered this, he looked thoroughly disappointed. I am sure that Londoners, especially artists, will be shocked by his words. It was not a very complimentary first impression. From my point of view, in spite of the weather's inconveniences, winter is actually the best time for visitors to come to London and have a look round. One can find far better and finer scenes to look at in some other places in spring, summer, or autumn, but one cannot see this typical winter except in London. I really hope my fellow artist can calm his mind and look again carefully at the winter scene in London. I myself find no other place and time so suited to my style of brush-work.

It is true that one can very seldom be spared from catching cold in London's winter. For my part, I always expect this affliction as soon as I know winter is arriving, and I have never tried to get it cured, for one is no sooner cured than the next comes. I just let it have its way. I have seen many a friend of mine being put to bed for a few days and hardly able to talk. Once I was advised to take some whisky with hot water and lemon before I slept, and

I was completely drunk, knowing nothing until the next morning. But I expect most Londoners must have their own patent remedy, and as it is such an inevitable event I tried to collect the names of cold cures from London chemists, but had to give up the idea eventually because I found there were too many of them to be remembered. In the daily papers not a day passes without an advertisement of some cure. I remember I had a talk in a hotel reception room with a lady who was trying to sniff up a few drops of hypochloride through her nostrils. As she closed her eyes and seemed to be going to sneeze, I could hardly help sneezing myself. It was like trying to stop a smile when someone else is laughing. She then said she wished someone could invent a better and quicker medicine for curing this nasty thing. I said I should be the richest person in London if I could find that out! It is so interesting for me to read London papers at this time of the year—— When I look at the photographs they publish I usually sneeze once in sympathy. I saw a news-reel some time ago that showed an office with forty or fifty people working in it in the morning while later in the afternoon there were only two left—all the rest had colds. While the sneezes sounded in the film here and there, many of the audience joined in. It is a typical sound in London at winter-time.

I dare say that I can observe English characteristics more easily and clearly in winter-time than at any other season. Although a number of modern houses have central heating nowadays, yet many families still prefer to have a coal fire, which is the fire I call "The first ancestor of our civilisation." I have been to many old English houses and the scene that sticks most in my memory is one of the host or hostess generally standing on the middle of the hearth-rug with their back to the fire. I suppose it is better to talk to all the guests and entertain them all from that point, but I wonder whether they realise they are hiding the fire from others! I myself love to watch the free play of the flames dancing and quivering, so I sometimes have to do so through the legs of the host. English trousers are very thin and tight and take up little space to be sure, but it is awkward if it is the hostess who stands by the fire! Once I made a most amusing observation of this habit in an old building at Finsbury Circus, where I used to teach. There was a big common-room for the staff and a good fireplace in it. While I was sitting at a table correcting some papers, one of our revered professors, slim of figure, with a bald head and white beard, walked straight to the fireplace. Turning his back to the fire and putting an eye-glass to his right eye he began to read very attentively. With his head and feet fixed in position, his legs and waist swayed slowly from right to left and then back. After I had watched for some time I half closed my eyes and tried to look at him again. I could not see his head and feet but only the moving part, which made me think of a great pendulum such as we find on huge, old-fashioned clocks. But I hope my readers do not think I am making fun of the professor! Professors are always to be respected, and I, especially, come from a country where we respect elders very highly. Now the place at Finsbury Circus has been converted into business premises and this interesting observation can be made there no more.

In China it is extremely cold in some parts in winter-time. We, too, have fires, but different sorts according to the district. In my native city, Kiukiang, we burn char-coal in a bronze basin on a wooden stand and it is generally put in the middle of the room for people to sit around. Nearly every room has one, but an economy can be made by moving the brazier from one room to another. It is no use for heating our backs, but we like to put our feet on the stand if it is not high. Our feet are often colder than any other part, since our shoes are not made of leather but entirely of cloth. If the stand is high, then we warm our hands over it. Anyway, sometimes the coldest weather is almost unbearable, but we have the advantage that it is always very dry and sometimes sunny too. I do not consider London winter weather is very cold compared with ours, but the air is so damp that it makes it oppressive and drives people to seek a change.

After being pestered by youngsters in the streets around Hampstead Heath disguising themselves and asking "a penny for the guy," once I went up the Heath to see what happened there on the fifth of November in memory of Guy Fawkes. They let off some fireworks and then burnt a dummy Guy. An old gentleman came up and spoke to me, and declared he wished he could meet the original Guy, for he would certainly make a good leader of the Opposition in the House of Commons. I only smiled.

During my first winter in London I was interested in the Christmas Eve services for English people and New Year's Eve for Scottish at St. Paul's; but my most curious experience at Christmas time was when I joined the Christmas shopping people in Oxford Street. As the crowds of Christmas shoppers appear every year they do not attract me any more, but they generally remind me of what we should be doing about this time of the year in my home country, and I cannot help dreaming about my own home far away. We Chinese are home-birds and it is the custom for no one to stay away if he can get back at this season. There are many folk-songs urging and persuading people to go back at the end of the year; I can only quote one of them here: *A Good Excuse for Students*—a verse we all know by heart:

Spring days are not for study,
Summer days are fine for sleeping.
When Autumn comes, Winter's on the way
When we pack up our books for New Year's homing.

We do not send greetings for Christmas, but we have a New Year's Eve gathering which is the chief festival of the whole year. By our calendar it takes place more than a month later than your New Year. It is the time when harvest is finished, our farmers are all at rest except for doing some hand-work indoors and our merchants are very busy making an annual account. The ceremony for this festival generally takes a few days and it is the only holiday in the year which we all have throughout the whole country. From New Year's day, every kind of business will be closed for some time, and we do nothing but enjoy and amuse ourselves in every possible way. Before it comes, every family is very busy making all sorts of preparation for it, especially making many kinds of preserved foods for at least a month's use. The richer and bigger the family the greater the preparations. As my own family had more than thirty persons living together under one roof, you can imagine how much we used to prepare for one month's use. When my grandmother was the head of the family, she generally ordered so much that there was still some left three months later. And the foods are preserved in many ways with special flavours, every family keeping to its traditional method. I cannot describe them all in detail here, but I can only dream of them for myself.

Although flower-shops in London still sell all sorts of flowers in winter, yet one

Winter-plum blossom

knows they are forced into blossom by artificial methods. In China, the winter-plum blossom is the flower most beloved by us all. We generally call it "The head of all flowers," because it blossoms before any other, and appears to have a very strong character which enables it to bloom in spite of the severe frost and heavy snow. It is my own favourite. I have collected hundreds of poems and paintings on it by our great masters and I myself like to paint it too. Once I wrote two lines about it when I thought of it with great longing here in England:

> *Not a flower in all this sea-country is my choice*
> *I only hope to have the winter-plum drift into my dream.*

I have not seen it for five years and I wonder when I shall again!

聖詹姆斯園中鴨結隊

游行泛綠波四圍樹木多

清風鼓舞興趣餐天和

水波一泓清澈底曾照雙

雙攜手過游游人已隔天

河鴨兮鴨兮汝無恙我自

臨風感呢名

亞

Translation of the poem is on page 6

London Fog

London fog is such a phenomenon, that I should like to devote some separate pages to it here. In an old number of *Punch* I found the following poem:

> *Thou comest in familiar guise,*
>   *When in the morning I awake,*
> *You irritate my throat and eyes,*
>   *I vow that life's a sad mistake.*
> *You come to hang about my hair,*
>   *My much-enduring lungs to clog,*
> *I feel you with me everywhere,*
>   *Our own peculiar London fog.*
>
> *You clothe the City in such gloom,*
>   *We scarce can see across the street,*
> *You seem to penetrate each room,*
>   *And mix with everything I eat.*
> *I hardly dare to stir about,*
>   *But sit supine as any log;*
> *You make it torture to go out,*
>   *Our own peculiar London fog.*

I think Londoners must often write ditties like this about their fogs!

"It was Whistler who discovered London," wrote the late E. V. Lucas, "as a city of fugitive, mysterious beauty. For decades the London fog had been a theme for vituperation and sarcasm: it needed this sensitive American-

Parisian to show us that what to the commonplace man was a foe and a matter of rage, to the artist was a friend. Everyone knows about it now." I do not claim to be more than a commonplace man, but as I am a Chinese who has lived in the interior of an Asiatic continent and been used to the mountain fog and lake mist for many years, I have a special feeling about it. Before I came to London I often heard of the London fog and never believed the comments. I think I have always had a good feeling towards mist since I was very young. When I lived on the top of my native mountain, I never found any joy which could compare with looking at the thick mist or fog rising up from the bottom to the peak; it seemed to swallow up me and everything at once. And the particles of it touching my face gave a very cool and refreshing sensation. But although I have many a time seen the morning or evening mist covering a whole city from a distance as we find frequently described in our poetry or painting, yet I have never experienced thick fog inside a city until I came here. The fog here is not the pure white colour I used to know, but yellowish grey and sometimes blackish. The particles of it do not strike the face with coolness and refreshment, but my nostrils detect in it the presence of smoke and a very oppressive air.

During my first winter here, a friend of mine wrote jokingly from China, asking whether the London fog really was as thick as pea-soup or able to be cut by a knife. I gave a negative answer as I had not then met it at its worst. On the next New Year's day, I was invited to attend a party near Gower Street. Having started out from Hampstead I was approaching Mornington Crescent when without the slightest warning the sky suddenly became enveloped in a thick, yellowish shroud, which grew still thicker in the darkness of the gathering twilight. I wondered why the day-time should be turned into night so soon, as it was only about three o'clock. Tempted by this strange sight, I got down from the bus and preferred to walk. Hardly seeing anything, I walked on the pavement and had many amusing adventures; once I struck a pillar-box, then I found myself clutching a man's hands; as we bumped into each other we broke into a laugh but could not see each other's face clearly. At last I thought a light in a shop-window was that of a bus coming nearer me very steadily, so I tried to avoid it by walking closer to the side and did not realise I was walking into a mews by the side of Maple's shop. I felt I had to walk on the way more strongly and heavily than usual, as if I had to push something which was pouring around my body. It was not only I who had to do so, but the buses had to move very slowly as if they were hindered by the same thing. A curious idea came to me that such minute particles of fog, when they were gathered together in a great mass, could be a strong factor in any sort of struggle. Individually they are nothing, a baby might easily catch them, but a group of the cleverest scientists would simply fold their arms helplessly before them in the mass. Is there really some mysterious power still in existence in the world? As the power of mass movement has been proved by this heavy fog, I wonder whether any man-slaughtering dictator or militarist would dare to face a mass of humanity!

Soon the sky became brighter and it was like a huge, yellowish-grey canvas in front of me. My eyes sparkled continuously and I just wanted to walk on and on without remembering the party. Occasionally I could see the faint images of people moving in Oxford Street, which I was gradually approaching. It seemed to me that the street was wider than before and there were more people there too. Although I knew quite well the sort of things people usually do there, I found it more interesting to imagine what they were doing under the fog than actually to watch them. When I am imagining I generally like to picture the attractive movements of humans—their gestures, their smiling, their coming and going. As they appeared to me in the fog, they were all lovely creatures, with nice-looking faces, very friendly, neither rich nor poor, carrying on their duties as they should be, without class or difference in age. I always think imagination could be the one great comfort of human beings nowadays, but people are losing their sense of wonder, so that is why they only see London fog as a foe or a matter of rage. For myself, it always leads me to imagine what life must lie underneath it. To be sure, a part of all human action should be hidden under a cover such as fog, so that it might be visible and invisible at once, and I think that is why London has a particular beauty, perhaps more than any other city in the world.

Suddenly I realised that I ought to be at the party, although it would last until seven or eight, but I very much wanted to read an account of the fog in the next morning's paper. On my way back, I bought a late final *Evening Standard* with a very striking heading on the first page, "Seven People walk into the River." The English journalist always has a great sense of humour! I read how a good many people were walking along the bank of the river Thames and that seven of them lost their way and walked into the river when the heavy fog came. At once I remembered a cartoon in an old number of *Punch*, which was a drawing of two shadowy gentlemen, one of whom had a top-hat and an umbrella and the other no hat but muddy hands and wet clothes, with the following lines underneath:

58

Befogged Pedestrian: "Could you direct me to the river, please?"

Hatless and dripping stranger: "Straight ahead. I've just come from it."

When I put the caption and this cartoon together I could not stop laughing, and then I wrote an amusing article for a Chinese paper in Shanghai. I began by saying that English people are fond of walking, in a way which we Orientals would be unable to imagine. They like to have a walk every day, it being almost as important as daily meals, and some might even consider it more important than meals. They walk in the morning, in the afternoon, as well as in the evening—almost any time in the day. They walk in the sun, in the rain, in the snow as well as in the heavy fog, despite any kind of weather. This is a typical English characteristic! Then I quoted the above news and the cartoon. But here I explained that English people were very fond of water too, and nearly every one of them could swim, so that the reader must not think all seven were drowned when they walked into the river. I ended the article by saying that as soon as they all emerged from the water they continued their pleasant walk home!

Once I asked a young Chinese girl to write a short essay about London fog in Chinese after she had only been here six weeks. I thought she might say the usual things, especially as she had come from Hong Kong. But she wrote that unlike many people who hated fog, she was very fond of it, because it was so mysterious and conveyed a sense of horror too. She then described a play that she had seen in London. In the play, a beautiful young lady was murdered during a heavy fog which made the whole place so dark that the victim could find no way to escape and so the murderer had an easy task. At the end of the essay, she commented from the traditional Confucianist point of view: "Why do those people like to act such an unbenevolent and unrighteous thing?" It was a surprise to me that she, at her age, should write like that. But at least the English reader may see that the Chinese are not at all unfriendly to their fogs!

Besides the thickest type of fog I have just described, I like almost any kind of fog unless I have grown very tired of it from its continuance over a long period. I was once taken up the tower of Westminster Cathedral, which is supposed to be the highest place in London and from which the whole city can be well seen. It was a semi-foggy day and when we were at the top we could not see very clearly into the distance. My English friend thought I was only trying to be polite when I said I liked it and he kept apologising that it was not a very good day for coming up. If it was fine, he said, we could see where St. Paul's, Greenwich Observatory, Kew Gardens, and all these places lay, so he promised to take me there again. Really I could not understand what he meant by saying that there was nothing to see that day. I thought I had enjoyed the view immensely. Is it such a great pleasure to be able to pick out the round dome of St. Paul's among all the chimney-pots? I think there is no profound enjoyment simply in picking out a place and giving it a name, without ever visiting it and knowing what it really looks like. Some time later I went up the tower again on my own. When I reached Westminster Cathedral the lift conductor advised me not to waste a shilling to go up and see nothing, as it was very foggy that day. I replied that I was wanting just to see nothing, and he smiled while he took me up. I was the only one there, and as I walked round all four sides of the tower I thought that I was living in heaven. I could

PLATE V. *Fog in Trafalgar Square*

not see the near-by chimney-pots underneath my feet and really had the feeling of having got away from London's noisy traffic for a while, although it was quite near me still. Through the vast white mist in front of me I could even imagine far, far away my remote home! This feeling of mine can be illustrated by quoting a passage from Dr. Lin Yutang's book *The Importance of Living*:

"I may suggest that there is a different kind of travel, travel to see nothing and to see nobody, but the squirrels and muskrats and woodchucks and clouds and trees. A friend of mine, an American lady, described for me how she went with some Chinese friends to a hill in the neighbourhood of Hangchow, *in order to see nothing*. It was a misty day in the morning, and as they went up, the mist became heavier and heavier. One could hear the soft beat of drops of moisture on the leaves of grass. There was nothing to be seen but fog. The American lady was discouraged. 'But you must come along; there's a wonderful sight on top,' insisted her Chinese friends. She went up with them and after a while saw an ugly rock in the distance enveloped by the clouds, which had been heralded as a great sight. 'What is there?' she asked. 'That is the Inverted Lotus,' her friends replied. Somewhat mortified, she was ready to go down. 'But there are still more wonderful sights on top,' they said. Her dress was already half damp with the moisture, but she had given up the fight already and went on with them. Finally they reached the summit. All about them was an expanse of mists and fogs, with the outline of distant hills barely visible on the horizon. 'But there is nothing to see here,' my American friend protested. 'That is exactly the point. We come up *to see nothing*,' her Chinese friends replied. . . ."

Perhaps this is one aspect of our mind which is very difficult for Westerners to understand. Is it really so? I suppose our aims are sometimes different. Westerners are usually more anxious to know a date or historical fact about a place or its name, so that they may describe it and talk about it with their friends, but we simply aim at enjoying the view and afterwards we rarely discuss our experience.

I have enjoyed the London fog in many circumstances. The morning and evening mists in spring and summer give a greenish colour under their veil when I look at the trees in the parks and on Hampstead Heath. In autumn the mist changes into a yellowish and reddish colour, but in winter it becomes grey or blackish. As its colour is always changing, it supplies an inexhaustible sight for me to look at and keeps my brush busy too. It is said that Turner reached his pre-eminence in the representation of the various forms and phenomena of the cloudy sky from living under the constantly changing foggy weather of London. And Whistler's *Old Battersea Bridge* betrays at once that he lived in London for a long time. Surely the grey and black colours in his portrait paintings of his mother and of others are especially the result of his London environment, which has so rarely influenced other English artists. Although the water-colours of Gainsborough, Cotman, and Cozens, display many misty effects, yet I think the brush and colours used by Corot would be the most suitable medium for the obscure London scene.

I too have tried to paint some London scenes in fog. Of course, I can only paint in water-colour, especially in monochrome. However, I find the London fog and mist have suggested many new ways of painting which we Chinese have been trying to use for centuries. In a Chinese landscape-painting a few spaces left blank suggests the fog and mist, but I myself have found sometimes that our great masters have specially avoided painting the foreground such as buildings and so on. After I had watched the London fogs very closely, I ventured to try the same method. When I showed one of my paintings *Trafalgar Square* (Plate V) in my third exhibition in London last year, I heard much talk about it. People said generally that it was a trick of mine to put only a faint image of Nelson's Column and a group of pigeons moving about underneath, and that the painting had not much work in it. It might be an excuse for me to say that I left the blanks there to suggest fog, but I just want to ask the onlookers whether they saw only blank spaces, or felt them to be not quite empty. Although it seems simple when looking at the finished drawing, yet I would like to know what kind of medium could be used for painting such a scene in details. If one is interested in seeing every detail there, I suppose it would be better to pay the place a visit! There are some more foggy scenes reproduced in this book, and I shall be interested to know people's opinions about them.

Somehow, I like to observe Big Ben and the Houses of Parliament in fog too. I generally go over to the other side of Parliament Bridge and look at them a little distance away from the river. Big Ben gives me an impression of immense height and the whole House looks so lofty and dignified because all the rest of the buildings around it seem to be lost to sight. The only way to look at this famous historical building is in fog or mist! If I may make a suggestion, I would like to see whether it is possible to abolish all the surrounding houses and to make them into a big recreation ground for M.P.s to walk and talk in, instead of in narrow lobbies. This would keep journalists and cartoonists very busy depicting them all the time. I have written a poem about the Houses of Parliament which will reveal my strange feeling:

The ancient building of Parliament is a lofty one,
Holding a high reputation in the West.
No matter how changeable are world affairs
It is always ready to deal with them.
But the atmosphere in the sessions can compare with the
*   weather,*
Always shrouded in thick mists and light fog!

It is interesting to know that we Chinese have been born to the love of fogs for thousands of years. Once I read a book on historical events, which spoke of a gentleman called Chang Kai of Later Han dynasty (A.D. 025–220) who was very skilled in Taoistic magic and could produce fogs whenever he liked. He lived as a hermit in the mountain Hung-Lung. As he was so famous for producing fogs, a great many people went to live with him and tried to learn this special magic, until the mountain which was previously a place without inhabitants, became a highly populated town. As it was always in fog and they produced fogs all the time, people who lived far from that place gave it the name of "Foggy Town." Whenever I

Chang Kai producing fog
from his mouth

write something to China or to the Chinese newspapers, I refer to London as "Foggy City." But although I have been here for five years now, I have not learned the magic for producing fogs yet! I would like to conclude this topic with one of my poems on London fog:

65

Oh, London fog, London fog,
How many people have pierced the fog's special joys
You want to go East, find yourself West, mind in utter con-
fusion.
This way, that way, all obscure—that is the road in fog.
Bumping shoulders, kicking heels, exclaiming merrily,
No distinction of fine and plain—that is the meeting in fog.
Morning and evening, best of all,
As if there, not there—that is the trees in fog.
I like their subtle, evasive manner,
That's why I like to live in London fog for a long time.

倫敦霧倫敦霧幾人參透霧中
趣欲東忽西意茫然來去不明
霧中路摩肩接踵共歡言美醜
何分霧中遇最是晨興夕照間
若有若無霧中樹愛汝神態太
依稀何妨長在倫敦霧裏住

寶城課詠

Translation of the poem is on page 66

London under the Moon

In previous chapters I have occasionally mentioned the moon and what she means to us. Since the publication of my *Lakeland* book, in which I stated my great love for the moon, I have often been asked by friends whether I saw her on this or that night in London. There is a moon in London sometimes, but it is very difficult to see her and still more difficult to enjoy looking at her, for London is so often cloudy and rainy that the moon hardly has a chance to show her face to us. I have been grumbling to myself about not seeing her much in these last few years, but probably she has been there all the same.

I doubt very much whether Londoners really care if they see her or not. There is too much rushing and hurrying to and fro in London day and night. Walking and even standing in the streets, I always feel an unsettled and un-restful atmosphere around me. This is probably the reason why most people who live here do not really stop to enjoy the moon's tranquil beauty, even if she is in sight. Perhaps, too, the moon herself prefers to hide her face in the clouds or only to shine dimly because of the many street lamps making the London streets as bright as day. As we have the traditional idea that people are easily attracted by false beauty and generally neglect the true, so it is perhaps that she is ignored altogether by Londoners. And nowa-days people are so crazy about living and dream so dreadfully of death, that they use cars instead of walking, draw blinds on the windows of their houses instead of going about outside at night, and shun the night wind.

The cool brilliance of the moon does not appeal very much to those who are always in the midst of excitement and thrills.

In fact, she does not want to be seen by people all the time. In China there is a legend which says that the moon used to be inhabited by two sisters, and that their brother lived in the sun. The sisters became very much embarrassed because people gazed at them so much, and asked their brother to exchange habitation with them. He laughed at them, and told them there were many more people about in the day-time than at night, but they told him, if he would change with them, they had a plan whereby they could keep people from looking at them. So they changed, and the two sisters went to live in the sun, and no one can look at them now, because if people try to look at them, the sisters immediately prick their eyes with their seventy-two embroidery needles which are the sun's rays.[1]

According to this story, beautiful Chinese girls do not want to be gazed at by many people! How strange it is! Besides, our people, especially poets and painters, have never ceased gazing at the moon since we realised her beauty. I have said in my first book *The Chinese Eye*, pages 107–8:

"Our poets and painters, you will find, are very preoccupied with the moon in their creations. In their own lives they are also moon-lovers: often they will bring wine-pot and lute and sit solitary beside a pine to enjoy the moon on a quiet night. . . . The moon rising at night is beautiful in form and mood; we love to paint her in our landscapes and to make her the companion of our poetry. Li Po's lyric to himself, his shadow, and the moon, is justly famous; in jovial mood he cries:

[1] Park: *Chinese Fairy Tales and Folk Lore Stories*, p. 6.

I lift my wine-cup to invite the bright moon,
With my shadow beside me, we have a party of three.

And Su Tung-P'o has almost identical lines:

Whom do I sit with?
'Tis the bright moon, the clear wind, and my own shadow.

Su was evidently a little less fond of the wine-cup!"

I could make a thick anthology of Chinese poems and stories about the moon, but I can only write briefly about her here. I must say that not everybody in China has the same degree of love towards the moon, although we are fortunate in being able to see her at least fifteen nights in every month. It is funny that some of us, when in trouble or in grief of vain longing to see somebody, go out walking under the moon, often trying to talk to her or even crying at sight of her beauty. I suppose there is bound to be some secret attached to every heart which cannot be told or is inexplicable to others. Why not tell the moon? In England I often read such a line as "my good-night look at the stars" which is always uttered when a mother is thinking of her child or a lady of her lover. Obviously they have not the moon to look at and turn to the stars. But even stars come very seldom on London's sky. Lord Byron has written the following two lines:

The moon is up, and yet it is not night;
The sun as yet disputes the day with her.

How very true it is in my experience in London! Whenever I see the moon rising before dark, I feel somehow disharmony in my thoughts. Then I realise that I am in a different climate from my remote home!

Although I often failed to see the moon in the Lake District, yet I have met her from time to time in London. One occasion about two years ago I shall never forget. It was very late at night and I saw the new moon, "silkworm-like" as we call her, just on the top part of my window while I was lying on my bed after long reading of Chinese poetry. I never draw the curtains of the window at night, so I could see her very clearly and closely. The chestnut tree outside the window shook its leaves, making changing patterns on the window glass after I switched off the lamp-light. I tried to remember some poems about the new moon, but none came clearly to my mind.

In London I can only enjoy looking at the moon some time very late at night. It is best after one o'clock in the morning and it is best of all in September and October, when the English call her harvest moon and hunting moon. I cannot walk very far from my lodgings late at night, because there is no night-service train or bus. Once an American lady friend of mine told me that one of her compatriots wrote that "only rich people are allowed to live in London because they can go about late at night in their own cars." This is very true. I do not mind being poor and having no car but I do mind if the policeman comes to disturb my tranquil walk late at night. One night I was attending a dinner-party in Chelsea and afterwards a friend of mine drove me home with him in his car. It was a very clear night and we were so late that the streets were completely empty. As soon as we reached Camden Town, I thanked my friend for having brought me so far and begged him to drop me there. Of course I did not tell him the reason why. At last he let me out so that I could walk and look at the moon on my way home, as I have written a line in one of my poems "*The bright moon escorting me home.*" On both sides of the street it was very quiet and there was nobody about. I did not know why I felt the moonlight was a stranger to those street lamps. And I felt her brilliance was stronger than theirs too—they were dwarfs in comparison. Once or twice I wondered if I was going to meet a policeman, because I had been told that they might come to ask me why I was walking so late and would take me to the police station. I did not mind their doing so if I could not find my way home—that would mean a shelter for me. Suddenly I saw a shadow coming out from a corner of the street in the distance. At first I thought it was coming towards me, but afterwards it disappeared. Then I came to Chalk Farm tube station. As I continued up Haverstock Hill Road, the moon shone on me even more brightly than before and I thought I was walking nearer to her step by step.

On another occasion I enjoyed looking at the moon on Hampstead Heath. It was one of the early days of March.

Under the moon

The weather was so fine in the day-time that I thought there would surely be a moon at night. So after dinner I went up to the Heath alone. Fortunately the moon was there and seemed to welcome me smilingly, although her light was not so bright as the electric lamps. I managed to get away from the lamp-posts and came to a bridge over a small pond. I could look at the moon in many ways, sometimes in the water, and sometimes directly through the bare branches of the trees. Occasionally I could hear the cry of the ducks, and the sound seemed to me as if they were sleeping or as if the baby ducks had something to say in their dreams. I could hear the birds cry from the trees as well, but certainly they were not singing as we generally interpret it. This kind of sound was not the same as they made in the morning. It was not high-pitched nor low-pitched, neither long nor short, just going on and stopping at times. I thought that might be the mother birds singing a nursery-rhyme for their babies. Yet it seemed impossible for them to do so at such a time, and I only supposed that the moon knew all about it. The place where I stood was quite near to Willow Road, where I could see cars driving past. I had an uncomfortable feeling as if the light of the cars were flashing by so quickly as to turn the quietness into vibration, so I tried to move up to the hill behind the pond. As soon as I got away from the road I did not feel the cars' motion any more. Then I thought of resting under a big tree, but when I approached it, I found an elderly gentleman sitting there, smoking a pipe. I did not want to disturb him, and found another tree to harbour me, but I was very glad to find someone with the same taste. It was a chilly night together with the cool brilliance of the moon. I felt chilly myself but I enjoyed the real tranquillity without even a single branch of a tree moving. I wrote a poem for this occasion:

> *The moon is not easily seen overseas,*
> *When I see her, how precious a time!*
> *I hum verses clearly in her presence—*
> *I let her clear light wash my heart.*
> *On every side quietness, and emptiness,*
> *To have you, moon, is a great comfort.*

There is another poem of mine written after I had been sitting by the Serpentine in Hyde Park on a summer night; it runs:

I know not if this is the scent of flowers or women's silks. . . .
The wind from the water-lilies how fresh and cool,
Breaking into fragments the moon's shadow in the lake,
Come flying down thirty-six mandarin ducks.

In Chinese thirty-six is a general number meaning a group and mandarin ducks symbolise lovers. I could not find so much quietness in Hyde Park even at night, as on Hampstead Heath, but that Park also is associated with my London meetings with the moon.

Last September, about the time of our mid-autumn festival, I unexpectedly received a letter from a young Chinese girl, whom I had known about ten years ago and had not met again for nearly eight years. She did not write anything but only copied the poem of Su Tung-P'o's which I quoted in the autumn chapter. At the end she added the few words: "If the moon has to be waxing, why should she be waning?" My thoughts went far beyond control and then I dashed up to Hampstead Heath in order to see the moon there. But she did not come out!

Translation of the poem is on page 18

London in Snow

The title of this chapter is misleading, because in these five years I have never seen London covered in snow. When I read Dickens's *Christmas Carol* and saw the illustrations for it I used to dream about London in a great cold whiteness, as Robert Bridges describes it in his poem *London Snow*, from which I quote the following lines:

When men were all asleep the snow came flying,
In large white flakes falling on the city brown,
Stealthily and perpetually settling and loosely lying,
Hushing the latest traffic of the drowsy town;
Deadening, muffling, stifling its murmurs failing;
Lazily and incessantly floating down and down:
Silently sifting and veiling road, roof and railing;
Hiding difference, making unevenness even,
Into angles and crevices softly drifting and sailing.
All night it fell, and when full inches seven
It lay in the depth of its uncompacted lightness,
The clouds blew off from a high and frosty heaven;
And all woke earlier from the unaccustomed brightness
Of the winter dawning, the strange unheavenly glare:
The eye marvelled—marvelled at the dazzling whiteness;
The ear hearkened to the stillness of the solemn air;
No sound of wheel rumbling nor of foot falling,
And the busy morning cries came thin and spare.
The boys I heard, as they went to school, calling,
They gathered up tne crystal manna to freeze
Their tongues with tasting, their hands with snow-balling;

Or rioted in a drift, plunging up to the knees;
Or peering up from under the under white-mossed wonder,
"O look at the trees!" they cried, "O look at the trees!"

When I first came across this beautiful poem, I read it again and again and my mind went far away to my home, because I thought it depicted my native city and not London at all. London has not shown herself to me like that and I wonder whether little boys and girls of to-day know how to gather up

"the crystal manna to freeze
Their tongues with tasting, their hands with snow-balling."

Perhaps this poem will presently be incomprehensible to London children!

It seems to me that London's weather has somehow changed in the last years. The continuous noisy traffic of cars running day and night prevents any "stillness of the solemn air," and the drowsy eyes of Londoners who are bewildered in their hearts with their heavy daily toil could hardly bother to marvel at the dazzling whiteness, even if such a sight were still to be found in London streets. Besides, indoors there are radios, the sound of the flame in the fireplace, people talking, laughing; and who would care about the snow "lazily and incessantly floating down and down"? I am inclined to think that after another hundred years of the present weather we shall need some scholar to explain this poem of Robert Bridges's in the universities. Lucky professors and scholars, who will never lack employment!

In *The Chinese Eye* I wrote some stories about the snow, and told how "Snow also is beloved of our people, and you may often find a snowy landscape-painting, or a snow scene in poetry. I have not seen much snow during my two years of London life, but I have gathered from newspapers and films that Westerners too feel a friendship for it, though they have a different way of recording this. They go out in ski-ing parties; the children have snowball-fights; everyone laughs and shouts with pleasure at the sport it makes! But we have a story about a poet called Meng Hao-Jan, who went out in the snow riding on a donkey and looking for winter-plum flowers." We also have a well-known phrase: "To walk slowly over the snow looking for poetic inspiration." I think we Chinese would be always in accord with Bridges's feeling about the snow! Now three years after I wrote that book I still cannot say I have seen much snow. It generally falls once or twice in a year, about the end of February. It can hardly be seen even when it falls, because the flakes are too small to differ much from raindrops, and they fall intermittently and never lie long on the roads. There may be a short snowfall, enough to make a thin layer covering the pavement or roofs, but it melts away very quickly again. Before Christmas, most of the shop windows are decorated with a snow scene and Father Christmas wearing a huge cap and scarlet coat comes along with a big bag of presents. I remember hearing a little girl of four or five saying to her mother as I passed them: "Shall we have snow like this at Christmas?- Why are we not having it now, Mum?" I waited for the mother's answer but she passed before I could catch it. I think this kind of question must have put a great many mothers into an awkward position in London!

One day about the end of February the year before last, a Chinese couple invited a group of fellow-countrymen to a Chinese New Year gathering. There were about fourteen people altogether and I was among them. We came to the house just after two o'clock. We chatted and laughed until presently, while I was talking with a friend, I suddenly saw a shower of white flakes falling down continuously outside the window. They were bigger than usual and occasionally fell down in rapid gusts, as they were blown by the wind. It was a beautiful sight that they formed, like countless thick, white strings or cords pouring down rhythmically as the strands on a weaving-machine, but they changed direction according to how the wind blew them. From falling in a certain pattern, they were suddenly blown into a different one by the caprice of the wind. Yet some flakes were reluctant to obey, and the most curious shapes and forms came before my eager eyes. Especially when the wind stopped suddenly or turned in another direction a group of flakes apart from the rest would hover in the air in a graceful manner, soon to fall down. . . . As I was so much attracted by the snowfall outside the window I did not know that my friend, who was short-sighted, was still talking to me, trying to explain to me some modern ideas. I did not realise it until I heard his wife scolding him for being so foolish as to talk to a man who did not listen to his words. I tried to apologise for my inexcusable rudeness in every way, but could not find any sympathy for my appreciation of the snow. Then I noticed it was still some time till dinner and I asked the host and hostess's permission to go out for a little while. I suddenly put on my coat and rushed out without giving any reason. I walked along the pavement and saw some snow remaining on the road here and there. The trams and people behaved as usual and they seemed not to have taken much notice of the snowfall. My idea was to see what was happening on Hampstead Heath. When I arrived there, it was not snowing any more. I waited for a little while, but no more fell and what remained disappeared too. Then I returned and the friends asked me: "What kind of nerves have you which drive you to act so madly?" I replied that I could find no snow on the Heath. They all burst into laughter and said: "You are a fool to want to see snow in London!" It seemed they knew quite well that London would not offer any good snow scene. I joined in their laughter—it was the only thing to do!

Anyway, I did once see a rather good snow scene on Hampstead Heath. It was one very early morning last March. Though my mind had been occupied with all sorts of unfortunate news from my country and my native home, I could not sit alone day after day with my grief, so I had tried to keep doing things as usual. After I finished some writing in the night, I felt a little tired and got up to add some coal to the fire. When I raised my head, I saw a kind of light outside the window and then walking near to it, found it was snowing. I would have shouted aloud if I had had nothing on my mind, even as it was, I was rather excited and went outside for a walk. It was the dead of night and there were no lights in the houses along the road except in mine, and the snow kept falling down heavily. On my hat and coat there fell a number of flakes, but they melted quickly. On my face I felt something cool here and there and I swallowed the flakes when they flew near to my mouth. After walking round a circle of the road, I got back and added coal to the fire. I was wondering how to see the snow on Hampstead Heath the next morning. But I had made an arrangement with some friends to go to Weybridge very early next morning. I kept peering out to see whether the snow was still falling and thought I had better not sleep in order to get to the Heath in time on the morrow, but eventually I fell asleep on the sofa. In my sleep I seemed to hear somebody calling me to get up and see the snow; I was terrified it would have stopped and gone completely without any trace. However, I got up about five o'clock and dashed to the Heath. There were no people on the road and I was delighted to think that I would be the first creature to tramp the snow. Yes, the Heath was indeed covered with a pure white blanket; though it was not very thick yet it was thick enough to cover the ground. On the tree-branches lay a thin whiteness following their forms, marking the clear outline of each one, and in the background and distance there were blackish grey mists against which they stood out still clearer. This made me review some of the well-known Chinese snow-landscape paintings by our great masters. Then as I walked to and fro by the edge of a pond I found many claw-marks of pigeons. Suddenly my face turned pale and I felt a sort of fire coming up from my chest, because I was so jealous of their getting here before me to tramp on the snow first! I could not reconcile myself to being forestalled and composed a very short poem to challenge the pigeons:

> *I did not sleep in order to see the snow;*
> *Who knows you got there first?*
> *I let you win this time,*
> *Please just wait until next year!*

Although I do not know whether I shall still be in London next year, yet I wish I could beat them. Then I examined the claw-marks closely and found that the pigeon had walked with its two feet following into one line, because there was no trace of two lines. I examined many marks, with the same result. Later I made some paintings of this snow scene and especially the claw-marks. (Plate IVa.) I remember the poet Su Tung-P'o has written a poem about the claw-marks of wild geese on the snow, which runs:

Who understands any place he reaches in life?
Man is like the flying geese tramping on melting snow.
By chance they leave some claw-mark there,
But the geese fly without caring whether they go East or
  West!

Since then we quote this poem to mean an incident in one's life in some place. As I am writing this little book, it might be considered as my claw-marks left on the London slush by accident!

I am sure many people in London will have seen the painting of *Fishing on a Snowy Day* by one of our great masters in the Exhibition of Chinese Art in London, 1935–1936. It brings a shiver to every onlooker and indicates the sort of snow scene we have. I do not suppose any Londoner has experienced anything like it. We in China like to boil snow for making tea, as our tea-experts say that it helps the tea-flavour to come out clearly. And our poets like to boil it to get inspiration for their poetry. But I must say that in the south part of China which is near the tropical zone, the people have never seen snow unless they have travelled far. There was a story written in a letter by Liu Tsung-Yuan of T'ang dynasty, which says:

"... I heard that in the southern parts of Hupeh and of Szechuan, it is always raining and there is very little sunshine. When the sun comes out the dogs will bark at it. I thought it was an exaggeration. But about six or seven years ago, I came

Dogs barking at snow

to the south. In the winter of the second year, there was heavy snow, which covered many districts of South China. And all the dogs of those districts were madly barking at it until the snow was completely melted. Therefore I believed what I have heard before. . . ."

It is interesting to see how rare things become so strange to the people who are not used to them, even to the dogs! Although there are far too many dogs in London, yet I have never seen one barking at the sun, which is rare enough here. Nevertheless, Londoners are most enthusiastic about the sun when it comes out! Snow is also very rare in London and Londoners do not even care. How strange! No wonder the dogs do not bark!

盡日清遊笑語頻
東風三月綠波生
送來槳帶溫存意
絕愛蜻蜓點水聲

蔚金特公園中遊船 呶 [印]

Translation of the poem is on page 7

London in Wind and Rain

Recently I read in *The Times* that:

"Weather is one of the world's mysteries. The study of its phenomena has not probed its secret. Where even the changes of weather are most constant there is no certainty. The monsoon may be early or late, and the rains heavy or light, and none can say why it should be thus one season and thus another. . . ."

This might well be describing the Londoners' worry, though it was talking about "Elusive Rain." It is interesting for me to read Lord Dunboyne's long-range "Rain Guide" in the daily *Evening Standard*, which seems to accept the inevitableness of rain in London. When rain falls, it is always accompanied by wind. But I have never felt the wind in London very strong, which is perhaps due to the closely packed high buildings; and the rain seldom falls in torrents. Though the wind is chilly, yet it refreshes me after the oppressive air of heavy humidity, and though the rain is gloomy, yet it cheers me up by showing me many scenes from a different angle. So I have made friends with both of them here.

I like to wander about in London parks when it is windy, because I can see the quivering shapes of the tree-branches and leaves being blown all in one direction or in confusion, producing a special sound very agreeable to listen to. Once when I took a walk by myself on Wimbledon Common one very windy morning, I came up to the horse

track facing a house with a windmill. On the right-hand
side there was a group of willow trees, and though I did
not find them very old and grotesque in the shapes of their
trunks and branches such as we generally like and paint,
they were rather pleasant to look at. They seemed to
have no main trunk, for in the Western way of growing
trees the trunk is generally cut very short near to the earth,
making the branches grow wide spread. These willows
grew in that manner and their long, slender branches
could not stand firm against the wind. I could see how
when it blew heavily from the right they all swept down
and bowed in the opposite direction. Some of them tried
to stand up but to little effect, beyond affording me a good
sight as they battled with the wind. If I did not look at
the leaves and the roots of these willows, I might mistake
them for a bamboo grove in China, because the long,
slender bamboos, when blown by heavy wind, generally
give this same effect. As these willows were not weeping
ones, their tiny branches were blown in a manner which
reminded me of bamboos with the young leaves just coming
out in the very early spring in my country. The willow
tree symbolises meekness and is a sign of spring in our
conception. When I looked at them here now, I remembered two well-known lines in one of our best poems,
which run:

Touches the clothes and wishes to make them wet, the apricot
rain;
Blows on the face but not cold, the willow wind.

Now on this Common, there were no falling petals of
any flower that might wish to damp my clothes and this
willow wind only gave me a shivery feeling as it was
nearly the end of autumn. I observed them very carefully

despite the fact that I might have been blown away if I had not planted my feet firmly. Afterwards I made a drawing of the scene.

"In my opinion," I said in my Lakeland book, "a walk in the rain provides the true opportunity of appreciating nature." I shall never give up this view even if I walk in the London streets in rain. I think the smoky, sooty surface of the walls of most London buildings do not bear close examination, but look beautiful behind the crystal-like rain-screens, which give them lustre. As I walk, the typical drizzle sometimes accompanied by gusts is blown in my face and brings an indescribable feeling; Londoners may show no sign of surprise as they are used to it, some may hate it relentlessly as it comes too often, and some may just take advantage of the wet to wash away the dust. Whatever they do I always find some pleasure in watching Londoners' faces in rain. Certainly they do not tell me that they like rain, but they are calm and unsmiling, which suggests that they probably have some objection to it. "It rains, rains, and always rains" cry many newcomers to London, but I would like to advise them to go to Picca-dilly Circus, Regent's Street, or the place near the Westminster tube station and look at the crowd of people holding umbrellas and waiting to cross the road in the rain. (Plate VI.)

I used to stand a little distance away from the crossing and watch them move about. I could not see their faces and bodies, but only the movement of umbrellas. If those had been made in dark blue colour, I would have mistaken them for the waves of the sea washing back from where I stood. Once I saw the Lord Mayor's Show by chance near Moorgate tube station. The rain was becoming gradually heavier and heavier. Nothing could be seen clearly in the procession, because most of the people in it were covered with canopies to protect them from the rain. Sometimes my view was completely shut out by the umbrellas of the people who stood in front, and I heard many complaints from other people too. Then I moved back behind the line of spectators and tried to look at the countless umbrellas. When I found a stand on the door-step of a big building I saw many umbrellas on the other side of the road too. As soon as the procession had passed by, the people on both sides suddenly joined together and swirled into a great tide in the middle of the road. I simply could not help crying out to myself, "Oh, umbrellas of London!" It was really a fine exhibition of umbrellas! I have also found it interesting to see one or two elderly Londoners holding an umbrella very firmly and sitting on a public seat under a tree in the parks, while the rain came down. Their eyes are generally cast on the ground, or gazing straight forward to the far distance, and their heads are as motionless as those of some wooden images in our local temples that generally have attendants to hold a silk umbrella in different colours behind the sitter. I almost bow to them as I did when I was young and took a sight-seeing tour in the local temples with my grandfather.

When I was practising rowing in Regent's Park one morning, I was caught by rain. But I just went on rowing without any change in mood, and it was quite strange to see how few people stayed on the water. It was a much better scene with few boats and it was a pity for anyone to miss such a lovely misty sight on both sides of the water. The trees were not very clearly visible but their different shapes were as clear as I like them. I always love the very thin, bluish-grey layer hanging above the water—very refreshing to the mind. So I say I prefer to be in London in rain rather than on a yellowish-grey, dull day. Afterwards I wrote a poem about the rowing:

PLATE VI. *Umbrellas under Big Ben*

A tiny boat emerges from the mist,
Light waves rock it unsteadily.
The cold weather has sent me the rain,
The sound of it is worth listening to.
The raindrops may wet my clothes,
But could not deprive me of enjoyment.

That night, I had to go round to visit a friend of mine in Golder's Green. It was raining still as I went out and still drizzling on my return. Somehow my personal feeling changed while I was walking to the bus-stop. It was curious to me to see a street lamp with a feeble dead, bluish light not lighting up any place but a very small circle around the post itself. Even the sound of the rain became very mournful in my ears. I tried to rouse myself by stretching my arms and holding my breath, but it had little effect on the surrounding atmosphere. When later I read a poem written by Thomas Hardy, I thought it could illustrate that night scene well:

While rain, with eve in partnership,
Descended darkly, drip, drip, drip,
Beyond the last lone lamp I passed
Walking slowly, whispering sadly,
Two linked loiterers, wan, downcast:
Some heavy thought constrained each face
And blinded them to time and place.

Oh, human beings are always human, never keeping one unchanging feeling towards any certain thing, but varying according to the mood and surroundings. Not very long ago, I was so full of worry about the war news in my native country as well as in Europe, that I just shouted out the following lines from the constraint and fear of my heart:

There is a stone in my breast hard to smooth away,
Who will draw water from the Silver River to wash the weapons
    of war?
There are many changes in Heaven as on Earth
Sometimes fine, sometimes raining, never unchangeable!

I cannot write any more about war.

It is strange that, though London suffers excess of rain most of the time, yet Londoners talk very anxiously of the need of it if there is a short drought. In my second year here I could not understand when my landlady told me she must not use the hose for watering flowers in her garden, because it was not allowed and there was a shortage of water. I tried to argue with her that I thought there was plenty of rain in London, and England was entirely surrounded by water, and so why should people be worried about the shortage of it? Now this year the same situation has arisen. Besides frequent warnings in the newspapers, I learned with great interest that Cardinal Hinsley, Archbishop of Westminster, had ordered prayers for rain to be said daily until May 21st in all churches and chapels of his see. Shortly afterwards it rained and rained continuously. One morning the maid came in to do my room and as we generally have a greeting about the weather, I suggested it was going to rain. She answered hastily: "Oh, we need it," which was hardly what I expected. Then she continued, "I am no friend of rain, but we have to pray for it because farmers want it badly." Another day while I was waiting for a bus at Euston Road, a gentleman stopped to talk with another who was standing by my side. The former said: "What a pity it is raining again." But the latter replied very promptly, "Oh, we farmers need it. It is worth millions to us." Merely saying, "I know," the former went on his way. Undoubtedly he must be a

Londoner. I am puzzled in my mind why the rain should be so obedient as to fall after the prayer!

It is a strange fact that we too pray for rain in times of drought. I must tell my readers that we generally have a very dry summer and always live under scorching sunshine for three or four months every year, or even more. According to the ancient customs, we offer jewels and brocades on the altars and beat the bells and drums at the summer sacrifices for the rain which is so vital for the crops. Later on, the local officials sometimes issue proclamations forbidding the slaughter of animals to conciliate Buddha. But a more interesting thing and one which I have seen when I was very young is the procession of group of Taoist priests to perform a supplication for rain on the altar in the temple of the Dragon King. The local god and the Dragon King are supposed to have the power of calling down the rain. The priests might be very busy performing their rites day after day without any sign of rain in the sky. Then the wooden image of the local god or of the Dragon King is taken out from its shrine and put on a seat, under the open, scorching sunshine too. This custom differs from place to place in China. Although the local people do not dare to say outright that they want to punish the gods by asking them to experience the dry heat as well as all the people, yet they are doing so for that very purpose. As soon as the varnished wooden face becomes sticky under the sunshine, the people say that the god is too hot and is perspiring; they add that this is the sign for rain because the god cannot bear the heat any longer. Yes, the rain always falls very heavily after a long time of dry heat! It is true in fact. Who can doubt the power of God? I think scientists make much ado about nothing and try to explain how the rains are formed from the water vapours which condense and fall in water-drops.

We Chinese are wind-lovers as well as rain-lovers. Not only have our men of letters written many poems and essays to praise both wind and rain, but both have been an inspiration to painters for centuries. Ma Yuan and Hsia Kuei are two outstanding painters of Sung dynasty, who excel in the execution of water-wrinkles and tree-branches to show the direction of wind. Mi Fei and his son, Mi Yu-Jen, of the same period invented a new method for depicting rain in torrents and drizzling. All good Chinese paintings have some hint of wind or rain. Not only is this true of landscape-painting; even if a piece of bamboo, pines or flower blossom is the subject, one always has an impression of wind or rain. Especially our great masters have told us that they liked to paint paintings in sight of wind and rain because their mood was deepened by them, and they could put more feeling on the paper.

One of our *literati* says that rain is a thing which can make the day short and night long. From this effect, all sorts of poetic inspiration come. I would like to quote one part of Giles's translation of *The Arbour to Joyful Rain* by the poet, Su Tung-P'o:

"My arbour was named after rain, to commemorate joy. Whenever our forefathers rejoiced greatly, they used the name of whatever caused their

The Arbour to Joyful Rain joy in order to commemorate the event. . . . Drought has been followed by rain; and to rain it is due that we are enjoying ourselves here to-day. Shall we then let its remembrance fade away? I think not; and therefore I have given to this arbour its name, and have added to the record the following verse:

93

Should the sky rain pearls, the cold cannot wear them as clothes,
Should the sky rain jade, the hungry cannot use it as food.
It has rained without cease for three days—
Whose influence was at work?
Should you say it was your Governor,
The Governor himself refers it to the Emperor.
But the Emperor says "No! It was God."
And God says "No! It was Nature."
And as Nature lies beyond the ken of man,
I dedicate this arbour instead."

This is only one example. There are many well-known halls called "Mild Wind" or "Great Wind" and so forth. These names have no superstitious connotation, but are simply chosen to commemorate the enjoyment of the wind and rain. I have inherited this habit, so I like London wind and rain!

一葉衛初暝微波
蕩不定清涼送雨
來琅々亦可聽而
僅濕我衣不能敗
我興 坐

Translation of the poem is on page 90

The River Thames

When I was a small boy, I heard of the English Thames, as it was mentioned in the children's text-book, but there were only a very few lines about it. I used to think of it resembling our Yellow or Yangtze rivers, and then dreamt of what would stand along the banks. Now I have learnt it is the only waterway in London. It may have been important, I suppose, for transport and trade in the old days, but now I take it to be a joyful river of pleasure. I have not seen one single junk or any big steamboat on it and its great function now seems to be to afford the people enjoyment. Oh, Thames, how many wanderers of how many nationalities have you seen through the past up till now? Does it care very much I wonder, about the changes and the business that *selfish* human beings have carried out in the buildings on its two sides? It will always be the same river forever!

Most Londoners, especially Englishmen, would find it very easy to tell the history of this or that bridge, how they were built and how much they cost. But these details do not stimulate a very stupid Chinese like me in the least! It is a big task to describe carefully the whole of the river. I am going to divide it into two parts, one near the city where buildings rise on both sides and the other nearer the country where both sides are lined with trees or only a few erections. From the account of my own character in the introduction, my readers would expect me to have no interest in the first part, but this is not entirely true. There are a number of places where I like to walk. For instance,

I may not like to walk along the Victoria Embankment in the day-time, because there is too much traffic and everybody seems in such a rush. I find it impossible to prevent myself from moving quickly if I am in an atmosphere where all are dashing along, and I believe this is a natural instinct, just as a young girl will move her feet when she sees a film of dancing. But after ten o'clock in the evening I can find here a lovely London night scene, although there may be trams and cars coming and going occasionally. I often walk there to and fro and find it interesting to look at the street-lamps on both sides, as they stand in their rows and are reflected in the water very close together. Usually I do not like many lights together, for they suggest rush, noise and excitement, but these many lights reflected in the water exercise a certain fascination on me. They are quiet and still if the water is very calm. When a breeze comes over the water, and the water-surface moves, then the lights reflected seem to me like candle-lights suspended upside-down. At other times a quivering candle-light would be annoying, but I find it a joy to look at these moving in the water.

Afterwards I like to walk up to the Egyptian monument and the two sphinxes. In the day-time, they do not give me a feeling of grandeur because all the noise of the traffic and the shining colours of buildings obscure them. At night, the other things are obscured but this monument and sphinx stand there immovable, unchangeable and everlasting. They have pride and dignified tranquillity. Of course they would be grand and still in this way if they stood in a huge, empty space as they once did in Egypt, but I presume they do not mind having been put here in the midst of confusion. I always think that anything of great value which has endured for thousands and thousands of years will continue to stand always, as it looked in the early days. Its greatness will never be spoilt or harmed even if it has to pass through sufferings or painful times. Any great civilisation will be the same! In front of this monument while I am passing, I feel myself very small—only a tiny dust particle of which it must have seen countless millions during the ages. And I also feel that it will just laugh at the struggle of human life and the present conflicts between nations. How many more it must have seen before European nations had names!

I also like to walk along the river in the day-time, especially in the early morning, along Millbank near the Tate Gallery. In front of this building I can have a very wide view over to the other side of the river and I can walk peacefully looking down to the river from the embankment. On this side, apart from the building of the Tate Gallery, I can see a huge building of modern architecture which is a contrast to the ancient one on the other side. In between them, the river seems to me wider at this part than at any other and it gives me a very big space across which to cast my thoughts. When I try to think in that sort of situation, I always feel myself expanding and relaxing. I must say the site for the Tate Gallery has been very well chosen!

The part where I love best to walk and which impresses me most is Cheyne Walk. I am sorry that I have only once been able to have a walk there in the very early morning. There were few people about and the morning mist covered everything which my eyes could reach. Albert Bridge seemed to be suspended in the mist when I approached it from a long distance and I was puzzled to find out how it was built. The most interesting thing is to walk there at night, best of all very late at night. I know several friends who live along the walk and in that neighbourhood. Luckily they used to ask me to dinner and I could walk there afterwards. Especially when I left my friend's house very late after dinner, I would not miss the chance to do so even if only for a few minutes. After eleven o'clock I could not hear very many cars and would meet few people on the pavement there. The trees generally hide the lamp-posts and the lights come out through the leaves or just behind or under them. These leaves appear the strangest green colour, which I do not suppose I could represent with artificial mediums. One night I walked there between the two bridges. I found a very artistic coffee-house along the road. It was not very big and only had a small window. Inside they had no electric lights, but candles. They had put one candle by the window which caught my eye and invited me to go in. But I saw nobody inside and I did not know the custom there at night, so I did not go in. It was very late. Another night I had a walk along there again. It was a misty night and I was attracted by the dim, mysterious surroundings and stood on one of the bridges for a long time. Then I ambled step by step in a very idle manner and forgot it was time to get back. It was a long way off from my place at Hampstead Heath but, though not easily, I did arrive home safely. Perhaps at that time most people had hidden themselves in their beds and hoped to have nice dreams.

One side of Battersea Park runs entirely by the river, where a short, stone wall has been built up the bank. There are many good trees planted there and no cars running. I went there one morning and enjoyed the walk very much. Leaning on the low wall, I could watch the graceful flying of the sea-gulls. They seemed content with their food and just swung around steadily in circles in the air. Against a background of misty grey colour, I could not see any other movement but that of these white-winged birds. Some of them tried hard to fly against the mild wind or they just stretched their wings and let the wind bear them higher and higher as if they were doing so purposely. Then I looked down on the surface of the water which seemed to me to be swaying slowly in the same direction as the gulls above. I could not help saying: "Rhythm is everywhere. Oh, the rhythm of nature!" In this park I like the lake particularly, where one can row, but the sound of trains and the smoke coming from two tall factory chimneys make me feel that I am not in a park at all.

The other part of the Thames I want to talk about is from Kew Gardens to Hampton Court and even farther. After strolling about in Kew Gardens for some time there is a very good place to sit and rest, by the side of the river. It is interesting; the trees leave a free space, and while I sit there I can listen to the sound of the ripples breaking on the water. In the distance on the other side of the river, there is a factory-like building with a trade-mark "lion" on its roof, which makes me even more aware of my surroundings through the contrast. Occasionally I can also hear the people walking along the tow-path, which gives a sort of rhythmic sound. I remember once I walked there too, as far as Richmond. It is very pleasant to walk that way and I cannot describe how joyful a time it was for me. I seemed to be walking along the water-side of a big stream in China, if I forgot to look at the buildings on both sides. I fancy that the scene there would be lovely in any kind of weather and season, and the interest always different. I have also thought that if there were a bright moon hanging in the sky with a very clear atmosphere, I would like to stay there the whole night, and there might be one or two white swans floating on the water to keep me company! I had another walk from Twickenham Station down to Kew Bridge from the other side and it was enjoyable too and will be always in my memory.

Then up towards Richmond, I have found many places

PLATE VII. *Deer in Richmond Park*

good for walking along the river-side. Perhaps the Cholmondeley Walk between two bridges is my favourite of
them and that a little farther away from the landing-stage
near Richmond Bridge is the next best. Standing on one
of the bridges for some time and looking at the rowing-
boats coming through underneath, I feel almost compelled
to move my hands in the same action. There is a road
higher up on the hills which leads me to Richmond Park.
I think walking there slowly one can get one of the best
views of the River Thames. Once I looked there far, far
away and thought the river was like an endless ribbon of
white satin spreading down from heaven and becoming
wider and wider to the part where it was divided in two by
a small island. The morning mist covered the island as if
it was a fairyland where I would like to live for the rest of
my life. It would be more than charming if I could ignore
the sound of traffic!

I had my first trip on the river when my friends, Prof.
Ju Péon, the Chinese artist, and Mr. S. I. Hsiung, the
playwright, went with me to visit Mr. Philip Connard,
R. A. who lives at Cholmondeley Walk. After we had been
shown most of his works, he took us out in a motor-boat
for a trip on the water. It was raining and I liked the
fresh smell coming from the grasses and water. There
were only four of us together with one engineer on the boat,
and I enjoyed looking at both sides where houses and trees
were completely woven into the rain as a Cantonese glass-
painting of China. Again Mr. Hsiung and I went to see
Mr. Connard on a summer day. After talking only a little
while, he suggested going out for a row. This time he wore
a sort of Spanish straw hat and no coat. He and Mr.
Hsiung rowed first and I sat in the stern of the boat steering
and facing him. As he was busy at his work, he did not
notice that I was trying to remember his rowing manner.

He looked very experienced, especially when he smiled with his lips twisted a little to one side. And then I had to change places. He sat in my place and just cried out: "In and out. In and out," because he thought we were not experienced in rowing. It happened that we did not often keep time with his shout- ing! It was a very fine after- noon and there were huge crowds bathing and swimming here and there along the side. The most interesting time I had on the river was when I rowed by myself once from Hampton Court farther up

A Chinese fisherman

through the mist. There it was very quiet and seemed to be completely cut off from the other part, and free from all crowds. Both sides were full of long weeds and I could hear the clear hissing sound of the breeze over them, pitched in the same tone as that of my boat's movement. At that very moment I could not keep from thinking of my early days in the town of canals, Soochow, which is called the Venice of China. There were many small rivers and streams around that town, and we could hire a boat for a month or even longer to go here and there as we liked. Outside the town we could see nothing except waterways, weeds, and ricefields. It was always a great joy to have a rest and know nothing about the world there. But now I do not know when I can have the pleasure of being there again! My English boat moved steadily with my thoughts. Suddenly a fisherman came into sight among the weeds, just drawing in his fishing-rod. How peaceful he looked and perhaps he did not even notice my boat or who I was. I wanted to jump out on the bank and tell him that I was a Chinese who had been used to fishing a great deal in my own country too. I kept thinking of this and that reminiscence; afterwards my thoughts formed into the following poem:

The grasses are green along the River Thames,
Falling petals puffed about reflect in the bright ripples.
A fisherman plies his rod with a merry smile,
Angling beneath the shadow of a willow tree.
The world is all business, but this fisherman takes his ease;
He lifts his head to watch the white clouds floating to and fro.
Suddenly a fish leaps up with waving gills and human speech:
"I wonder why you, fisherman, should act so cruelly!
On the surface of the water there are hoards of boats and
  steamers,
And I have no peace from the grinding sound of machinery.
I escape here to find a congenial place,
But now again I am tormented by you!"
Alas! The whole universe is full of murderous feeling!

翠煙起處若層巒
並坐深林向晚看
怕是夕陽欲歸去
萬杉風雨逼人寒

游愛平森林 呃

Translation of the poem is on the top of page 34

PART II

London Life

About Children

After I arrived in London, a friend of mine put me up in a house near Regent's Park Road. As I knew nothing about London then, and as my friend was busy most of the day, I sometimes just sat in my room and looked out through the window to watch the people passing. Once a little girl of about four or five came to the house opposite. She had a small stick in her hand with which she knocked at the door, for she was too short to reach up to the knocker. Then she stood there for about a quarter or half an hour and seemed to have unlimited patience in waiting for the door to open. She played gracefully with her stick and looked up and down the road. As long as she stood on the doorstep, I could not take my eyes off her. She was very pretty with her little rosy face and her bright green frock. I could not describe how much I was attracted by her and she gave me one of my very first impressions about London. "Does this child come from a very well-educated family or is she simply an unusual type?" I kept posing myself with all sorts of queries about her and eventually my friend told me that I should not wonder about such a common sight too much, otherwise I would never have any time for anything else in London. But I have a real passion for children, I have always been interested in studying their actions and manners—the results of training, upbringing, and national discipline. At this point I cannot help thinking of the influence of mothers especially, and of education! There must always be a difference between English and Chinese because we are brought up in such different traditions and environment. Even our houses are built in a very different style—except in Shanghai, Tientsin, and some other big cities—and our entrance gates are generally kept open all day long and so there is no need to knock for entrance. Brothers, sisters, and cousins, always live together under one roof, so we do not need to look for other companions. I hope my readers will not be surprised if I tell them I was not allowed to go outside the great entrance gate until I was over ten years old! The explanation is quite simple; our house is built on one level and occupies a very big space including several courtyards and a good garden. There are quantities of rooms in which to run about and vast space for walking. And in our estate we even had a small school building inside the garden, as my family is very big and I am the sixteenth child in my generation. Inside the big gate we could enjoy all sorts of fun.

This little girl reminds me of several things I have noticed about the English family. She is certainly one who has had a good upbringing, but is probably an only child, or one of two children. I often wonder whether such terms as "brother," "sister," "uncle," and "aunt" will be in existence in England after a few more generations if English families continue to decrease. Once I read in a paper that "people are more anxious than they have ever been to give their children the best possible chances in life, and they are inclined to be afraid of the increased responsibility that a large family must bring." This is a reasonable fear. However, most English children of the present generation still enjoy very much shouting out "uncle" or "auntie," as I hear in parks whenever I meet them.

I always find interest in watching children's actions and manners, and try to think of what I should have done at the same age. It is curious for me to realise that I shall

PLATE VIII. *Seagulls in Regent's Park*

never do these things again. I always like to see small children feeding birds in London parks. They have a natural love for birds, but they have the sort of possessive love which makes them like to get hold of them or touch them. Yet they make diffident gestures as if they dared not do so. In my observation, when children take out a piece of bread or food, they like to give it themselves to the birds. But as soon as the birds come near their hands, they suddenly throw the food away and give them a fright. Afterwards they smile or laugh as if they asked forgiveness. Oh, this smile touches the very bottom of my heart! Would I do the same? That I cannot tell. But I have seen many people in various situations trying to smile in hypocrisy, which also touches my heart with agony!

Pigeons and sea-gulls are abundant in the parks. Pigeons seem used to taking food from human hands and sometimes even like to alight on them as well. This attracts youngsters very much as I can see by their sparkling eyes. Sea-gulls give them the same excitement. But these usually swoop overhead and come down in groups of four or five at once. They seem very fierce and try to snatch up the food as quickly as possible. I have noticed once or twice a small girl of about six holding up a piece of bread with both hands over her head and then lowering it, seeming very much afraid to look at the gulls. As it was a lovely scene for my brush (Plate VIII) I almost went over to her and wanted to ask her why she liked to feed them if she was afraid. But I did not want to disturb her and watched her till she managed it in the end. She might be shy or a coward, but undoubtedly she loved to feed the gulls. I shall not try to explain the conflict between love and fear in her attitude, yet I think her face expressed as much in a natural way. As soon as we begin to grow up this kind of natural reaction begins to fade away!

I find the conversation between London children very entertaining. Whenever I can overhear them I always try to stand near without being noticed. I hope they will not think it very rude of me to do so, because I believe they have no secrets to conceal as grown-ups have. Once I was sitting in front of two small girls on the top of a bus and could hear almost everything they said. They discussed first the pictures they had seen and where they had been, choosing very exact expressions for what they wanted to describe and speaking in a soft, clear tone. Before they finished their talk, I thought I heard one of them say: "That's all I've done lately," and the other replied: "I think we are lucky to be able to do what we like now, don't you?" If I had not seen them and guessed their ages to be under ten before I sat down, I would have thought they were two grown-ups. At another time I was particularly attracted by three boys in top-hats who sat opposite me in an underground train. Each of them had a small case and an umbrella, and all looked only a little more than ten years old. One sitting in the middle wore glasses and took out a book to read. Then he said to the others: "I don't know why I still can't solve this problem." The one on his left looked at the book and remarked: "I couldn't do it either. I think it needs a calmer mind." But the third one on the right joined the conversation with "Sometimes the calmer mind does not help much in solving an abstract idea." As they picked up each other's ideas, I suddenly felt startled and decided I was facing three scholars and philosophers! Although I had no idea as to what they were talking about, yet I felt myself very vulgar before them. They were still being given in the school the good teachings of the past, but they did not realise yet that we have been carried far away from what we were taught in our younger days. They discussed the calmer mind.

They discussed the abstract idea. Could we grown-ups do the same now? Probably we are being warned how to wear a gas-mask or told to be ready in case of emergency. My own brain has been engraved with a thick mark "war" for a long time! I do hope and pray that these merry London youngsters will never grow up and be able always to talk about "doing as they like," "calmer mind" and "abstract ideas." As a whole, I find London children's talk very gentle and courteous, and especially natural and original. Although they may be copying what they have heard from their parents, yet one or two slips in their talk both amuse and delight the hearer, because they are always sincere in what they are discussing.

Being a foreigner in this country, especially one with a flat face and almond eyes, I could not escape the many street children who come up to ask for cigarette cards or about the "time." However, their intentions are good and they only want to hear me speak a word or two. I generally give them a smile as well. Four or five years ago, I used to hear them singing a chorus from the play, *Chu Chin Chow*, when I passed them. Once a compatriot of mine and I met a group of children on our way home who began to sing that as we passed. My friend was very much annoyed about it as he did not like the play at all and even began to lose his temper. I could not help laughing at him and said that they might think the song was a great compliment they were paying us. For some reason this chorus is not sung any more now!

One of my neighbours a few houses down the road has two daughters: the elder is about six years old and the younger about four. I used to see them walking along with their mother when my friend and I passed by, and they always gave us a smile. After a time we became friends. Their manners in walking were beautiful. They did not run about quickly and talk loudly. Afterwards we often invited them to tea. Sometimes their mother came with them, and sometimes not. One day the elder one came to our house and sat with us for a while. Suddenly she took my friend's hands and wanted him to go downstairs with her. They went outside and walked in a circle around the house and came up again. I asked her what she was doing. She told me: "I wanted to take a few minutes' walk." She said this sentence so sincerely and gravely that I could think of nothing in reply. But I supposed she took this walk every day, and felt she must not break the habit. They moved away three years ago, and I have not seen them again.

A friend of mine, Mr. N. L. Carrington, has three children. One evening he and his wife asked me to coffee. As soon as I arrived they told me that their children would not go to sleep until they had seen me, because they had heard I was a Chinese. I was taken up to see them while they were lying in bed. I talked with the two little girls of eight and five, but the little boy was too young and was asleep already. The other day I asked them to tea. They came with their mother punctually at the time I had said. The second girl, called Ann, brought me two of her paintings as a present. She described them to me and told me that in one drawing some people were coming along, then went upstairs, had tea and afterwards went out for a walk. The drawings were intelligent for a child, and I thanked her heartily. The two girls sat together in one chair and were helping each other. I offered them tea one by one, but Ann told me that she preferred cold water. The little boy called Paul, about three, did not sit quite so quietly as his sisters. He was a very healthy young person and played all sorts of gymnastics on the floor, causing us to laugh. He had his cup of tea too, but he did not seem able to manage the plate for his cake and sweets. I knew he would like to imitate his sisters, but he simply could not do it. Presently I offered another sweet to Ann. She hesitated a little while and then chose one. But she seemed not to like it and looked at me cautiously to see if I noticed her trying to wrap it up in a piece of tissue paper. I discreetly looked the other way. It was delightful to watch her natural shyness and awkwardness. It reminded me of a very similar predicament I was in a long time ago when I was taken to a relative's house by my grandmother. Unfortunately one of my cousins made me blush by pointing out my manœuvre. I think I treated Ann wisely and as soon as she got the sweet out of the way, we talked cheerfully in order to make her forget the trouble.

I am also very much interested in the education of children. After I had been here about a year, I took every opportunity of visiting schools for boys and girls. Once I was taken to see an infant school by my first landlady—she was the headmistress. When I got there, the children all stared at my alien face and seemed terribly inquisitive. They behaved exactly as they were told, but none of them would answer me a word but only smile. Then I was taken to the boys' and girls' department of an elementary school. After going from class to class, I made good friends with them all. Afterwards I was asked to attend their "Parents' Day." I really felt very awkward when I was put in a chair among the prominent people, where not only the children stared at me, but the parents as well. This made me feel like one of the human oddities on show in the Olympia Fair! I was sorry I had not brought photographs of myself to sell there! In another school I was honoured by a lady teacher who suddenly called up her students to point out the national flag of China. One of the girls pointed to a flag with a dragon on it and all

clapped. I thanked them heartily, and I did not want to spoil the whole cheerful atmosphere by pointing out that it was a flag of our last Manchu dynasty. After I got home, I wrote a letter to thank the teacher and tried to explain that China had become a republic and had had a new flag for many years now.

As a whole, I think Londoners show every sign of their interest in children. Apart from seeing signs of affection towards them in parks and streets, I have never ceased to study the advertisements and reviews for children's Christmas books every year! How many authors there are in London! I like Mr. A. A. Milne's work very much. Besides, there is a Children's Hour in the daily broadcast and a Children's Zoo. Again schools often have one free afternoon for teachers to take pupils to visit all kinds of museums and galleries, though in this connection I agree with a friend of mine, Mr. Herbert Read, when he wrote in *The Listener*: "A Michelangelo or a Rembrandt did not paint to amuse little children, or even bored adults. He painted because he had something serious to say to men and women of refined sensibility and mature intelligence. . . ." Children are apt to treat great works of art with flippancy and lack of comprehension, if they are brought to see them too young.

We Chinese here usually have some difficulties in finding a place to live in, because some might not like to take foreigners and some do not want to have children. So Chinese with families have particular embarrassment. At first I did not understand this at all. Once I went to visit a friend in company with a married couple and a child in a pram. As soon as we reached the house, the landlord refused to let the child in as he said that "No children" was in his agreement. We were all surprised because we had never heard of such a thing in all our experience at home.

I was even more surprised than the others, because I have the belief that everybody must remember his own childhood and must think of that time affectionately. Apparently this is not true. I looked hard for the reason for this unnatural action, until I was suddenly enlightened by reading a cartoon of three children in *Punch*, which runs:

"*Pat* (play-acting): 'Have you lodgings to let?'
Barbara: 'Excuse me, have you any parents?'
Pat: 'Yes.'
Barbara: 'I'm 'fraid we *never* take in children with parents.'"

This gives me the idea that this sort of prohibition must be rather common in London. But why object to children? Oh where is their sense of "give and take"?

Shyness and something like a sense of fear seem to me to be born in young children's minds whenever they meet a new thing or person. London's children may be better in this respect than those of any other neighbourhood, because they are used to more variety. But I also think there is some difference in individuals too. I know most Chinese children would not dare to answer questions from foreigners even though they tried to speak the Chinese language; and some of them will gaze at foreigners with great curiosity and smile in watching their actions. I had the same experience being a foreigner here. But the manner of London children talking to their parents or elders gives me a surprise when I compare them with what I would have done in my own younger days. For instance, I sometimes hear a boy of seven or eight shouting out: "Daddy, I don't think you are right." It is quite a reasonable expression which nobody will make any fuss about. But the first time I heard this I wondered to myself how a boy could address his father like that, because we are generally taught not to criticise our elders and especially not our parents. As we are virtually controlled by the Confucian idea, our elders enjoy the privilege of being respected by the young, and it is said they have more experience and therefore more wisdom. According to our ethic of "filial piety," our children are trained not to argue with their parents and upset their feelings, for this would be considered as "not filial." If a young person is insubordinate, he has not an easy position in society. So our children have won the habit of naturally accepting what they are told by their parents. After all, no parent would deliberately lead his children on the wrong road. Of course, it is a disputable point, but such has been the idea we have inherited for centuries. I do not think we should never be allowed at all to say anything contradictory to our parents or elders. When we are grown up, we may address them as follows: "Yes, father, but I think it will be better if we do it by another method." As a rule there are many obstinate parents in China, perhaps even more than in England!

I have heard older children in London discussing their parents and using such expressions as "We are very good friends," or "She or he is very friendly to me." There are many kinds of friendship of course. But I am often puzzled at this word being used between children and parents. Although the Oxford dictionary has defined it clearly as: "One joined to another in intimacy and mutual benevolence apart from sexual or family love," yet it seems to me to be used differently nowadays. Parents and children are naturally bound to be together for some time at least, and they have an instinctive love for each other with no time limit. Children may not like their parents when they are told to do this and that, but no normal parents would develop hatred of their *own* children. Even in China, some of our best scholars have strictly criticised the ethics of "filial piety" because they said children were not originally born for the sake of their parents. Yet we all think that children have been very well cared for by the parents after their birth, so they ought to be good (I mean here more than a friendship) to them in return. The word "friend" between parents and children, is a bond which I am inclined to think might be broken after a time. To me personally, the link between parents and children is unbreakable, also that between brothers and sisters. There is always something more than friendship in these links. So far we have not come to live under the strain of the entirely mechanically arranged life towards which modern civilisation is tending. Later on, my conception on this point will have to undergo a change! I think we shall then simply become original animals again, and as soon as the child grows up, he or she will run away.

All the same, we Chinese do not always consider the elder's thought is the best and the children's less clever than theirs. Let me conclude this subject by the following story. It is said that when Confucius went out in a carriage driven by one of his disciples called Tzu-Lu, they came to a place where they saw a group of children just building a small city-wall with odd tiles and bricks in the middle of the road. So Tzu-Lu

Confucius says: "We had better go back"

118

shouted out: "Keep out of the way and let us pass!"
But the leader of the children suddenly stood up and
said: "We will let you go if your master can answer
my question." "What is it?" Tzu-Lu asked. "Should
the city-wall be destroyed to let the carriage go or
ought the carriage to return if it cannot go through the
wall-gate?" the boy stated. Tzu-Lu was always very
rough in his personal actions though he was a sage, and
grew angry with this boy for asking such a nonsensical
question, so he tried to drive on. But he was then stopped
and Confucius said: "We had better go back!" Our
children are even cleverer than Confucius sometimes!

憂雨作奇藹園爐橢
閒語我數東方珍寶
閒爐處唱雨此談米
休乎生森此待

夏日園爐

Translation of the poem is on page 23

On Books

I have a great admiration for Londoners in the matter of books. In the streets I notice most of them walking about with books under their arms, and they even read them in the buses, trains, and tubes. I have visited many friends' houses, both humble and well-to-do, and nearly everyone has a library of sorts. When I went to tea with a grocer friend of mine, whom I know well and who lives at the corner of my road, I saw a number of books there and he told me he wished he had more time to read. What an admirable thing that even a working-class man has that sort of outlook! It makes me think of my own country and wish everyone of my compatriots could learn to read and enjoy doing so. England has gathered the great fruits of "compulsory education." I was told that when this new educational system was brought up for adoption there was a great conflict of ideas and opinions, and now everybody is grateful for it. Of course all readers have a different degree of appreciation, but I admire in anyone the ability simply to enjoy reading for itself.

In a speech at the 148th anniversary dinner of the Royal Literary Fund, the Duke of Kent said:

"I have always liked reading, and it is one of my chief regrets that our modern life does not give us more time for it. I often envy the gentleman of leisure of the eighteenth century who was able to build himself a magnificent room in which he could place his library and where he was able to sit in peace and enjoy it. He really could read and think carefully of what he was reading, knowing that he had ample time. To-day we read the first and last sentences of each paragraph and talk about the book as though we had studied it profoundly. . . ."

He made some criticisms of the production of books, but I only wish he could suggest a plan for having time to read in the way he said was so desirable. Everybody is always saying they love reading but that there is no time for it. I cannot help asking what has happened to people's time. If other pleasures take the place of reading books, it means this kind of enjoyment will cease to exist. If modern life does not give time for enjoyment, what is the use of it? I quite agree with the duke in what he said, yet there must be time for reading I feel sure. The very title of "six-minutes short story" in the *Evening Standard* only makes me feel more rushed and nervous, in keeping with London's atmosphere. Why should it last six minutes only, not five or seven? Perhaps there is no other man stupid enough to ask this question!

London publishers produce thousands of books year after year. According to the daily papers, it seems to me that there are new books coming out every day or rather, say, every hour or even every six minutes. Although the publishers do not intend their books to be finished in six minutes, yet they would probably be quite glad for the readers to finish reading in that short time and then buy a new one. The Duke of Kent is not the only one who has found that literature as an art is faced every year with the increasing danger of being swamped by commercialism; even publishers themselves feel the same. A publisher friend of mine once told me that his firm had no wish to produce quantities of books at high speed but that the public forced this policy on them. Another said to me that part of the trouble arose from the fact that people now-adays wanted to buy books for presents, not for reading. Ah, I understand now why they have a special "Christmas Sale"! I ask myself: "Isn't it better from the commercial point of view to expect people to buy books for presents rather than for reading?" I understand more and more the conditions of publication in China at the present time. In the old days we very seldom dared to write a book and it was very difficult to get it published. In the first place, when we write we have to use a special kind of style which sinologists call the "Chinese written language" and which is different from the spoken language. The difference does not lie so much in the words themselves as in the style or construction of sentences. In this written style, we consider the shorter or more concise the sentence the better it is. It goes without saying that long practice is needed before one can express one's ideas in book form. As the style is so concise, it takes many years of writing to compose even a thin book. Further, we get no royalty from books published and generally we publish them at our own expense. In the end, most of our ancient authors seldom saw their works published, because by the time they had something written ready for book form, they were generally too old to see it through the Press. Most old Chinese books are published by their authors' descendants or disciples. Although the process of publication was so difficult in those days, yet we had countless books in print. For instance, the Chinese Encyclopedia contains 10,000 volumes. But recently our publishing world has come to be commercialised as in any other country. It seems to me personally that it has driven us into making a change in our style of writing. Now we write books in the same way as we talk —we write down as many words as we would speak. If written work is paid according to the number of words, the

Chinese old style of writing would never be profitable. So this kind of change had to come! When we are not at war, our publishers turn out nearly as many books as yours. I should emphasise here that we now appreciate the new style of writing as much as the old ones and we think the former helps the latter in many ways. But strangely enough many sinologists do not attempt to read our new type of writing which is really easier for them, though we try to read modern English rather than Chaucer. Instead they like to stick to their privilege and remain distinct, priding themselves that they can read the "classical Chinese." How wonderful it is! But what a wrong conception of Chinese literature must be given to the whole world!

"No young people in former days have had to face such a mass sex-appeal as is evident to-day in *books*, plays, music, and, above all, in the cinema," says Dr. Drummond Shiels. I am specially interested that he mentioned *books*. Apart from Dr. Shiels' feeling in the matter, I wonder whether the use of sex-appeal is a debatable point. As I came from a country where sex-appeal was very strictly prohibited in the past, I was first rebuked by my friends when I expressed surprise at its use here. They told me: "That is beauty, that is art, and that is the thing that people are interested in." I could only nod my head without saying a word. But I want to tell Dr. Shiels that this kind of mass sex-appeal has gone to my country too. It travels everywhere as if it controls the whole world. If it has such power, why should it not be mentioned in *books*? Besides, I have watched another interesting point about the London publishing world. Publishers seem to encourage authors strongly to write on the topical subjects as if they were journalists getting news for papers. And publishers, authors, and journalists seem to work together to cater for a public avid over current events. For instance, during the Italo–Abyssinian war, a vast number of books came out on Abyssinia as well as on Italy in about six months, and then on Spain, Austria, China, Japan, Germany and now Czechoslovakia, and Poland. It seems as though, if there were not so many aggressors, publishers, authors, and journalists might die from starvation! It's an ill-wind that blows no one any good! And there are always plenty of incidents and crises cropping up throughout the world. Apparently publishers, authors, and journalists will never want for a living!

Referring to the journalists, I would like to extend my admiration to all London papers. Truthfully speaking, I enjoy reading them all, for their depiction of various voices in the human world, as varied as human faces. I am especially grateful for the Sunday papers which give me something to do on dull London Sundays. "Almost everything in the newspapers," says Mr. C. E. M. Joad, "is to some degree untrue by omission, exaggeration, distortion, and selection." But I suppose not everyone reads papers and believes them entirely. And this is a fact which all editors know very well. It reminds me of an old Chinese saying on books: "If you believe entirely in books, you had better have no books at all." The modern world gives a very sound proof of this.

There is also an ancient Chinese parable which tells:

"On his return after three years of studies abroad, a native of the Sung State (one of the Warring States) called his mother by her name. 'After three years' education,' asked the latter, 'why do you come home to address me by my name (contrary to the etiquette of our forefathers)?' 'The most virtuous, in my opinion,' replied the son, 'cannot excel Yao and Shun (two excellent emperors in our very ancient time). They are both called by their names. Again, I venerate heaven and earth above all, and these are both names. Now you are not any more virtuous than Yao and Shun, nor any greater than the universe. I think I am justified in addressing you in the way I did!' 'My dear son,' retorted the mother, 'do you think that you can practise to the very letter what you have been taught? I wish you would leave my name alone. For there are certain principles which, though mentioned in books, should not be acted upon. Hence you had better desist from pronouncing my name."[1]

This son certainly thought that he had studied books intelligently, and was paying high respect to his mother, but he did not foresee the attitude she would adopt. Oh, do books really help the conduct of human life or does their utility depend entirely upon the reader? Although people acquire much miscellaneous knowledge from books, I doubt whether many people really benefit from them. I can frankly say that I have not got much from Plato's or Aristotle's or Descartes' sayings when I have tried to read them, because I cannot identify them with my environment. In the same way, I am sure that no Westerner can get very much from Confucius's sayings (though many translations of his have been published), apart from the few who have especially studied Confucian ideas like those sinologists who are teaching this idea to many promising students. Confucius says: "If you know it, say you know it; if you don't know, say you don't know. That is really 'you know'." Now, how few people will say that they do not know everything Chinese if they have been learning it?

But anyway, to read books is always a great joy in life.

---

[1] Translated by Dr. Kwei-Ting Sen.

Some people talk about the art of reading, but I do not worry about that. I only like to read for pleasure whenever I have time, and do not care what it is. I find everything written worth reading, from one point of view or another. While I am deep in a book I forget drinking, eating, and sleeping. My room in China was always untidy, with books all over the place, and my family were generally very cross with me about it. Once, when the servants came and tried to carry all the books off my bed, I told them that I wanted to be buried in books. Eventually I was nicknamed "bookworm" and nobody tried any more to reform my ways. I have not become any better in keeping my books orderly since I have been here. But the maid and I understand each other and both benefit, because she need not do much tidying and I am spared interference. Once I gave the name "bookworm" to an English friend of mine, but she was annoyed by it. "One man's meat may be another's poison." I myself am quite proud of it! I daresay I put on a very funny face or gesture while I am reading, for I often notice that Londoners who read books in trains or buses generally adopt involuntarily expressions totally different from their natural ones. When I see hollowed eyes and two deep thick lines from both sides of the nostrils down to the corners of the mouth I feel that I am looking at a very serious reader. Sometimes a short-sighted gentleman may turn his head repeatedly from left to right and read with the help of a small magnifying glass close to the book. This makes me think about my own movements again. When I read a Chinese book, I move my head up and down repeatedly and from right to left, because our book is printed from the right to the left of each page and vertically. An American friend once said to me that Westerners were always complaining that the Chinese did things the wrong way round—from right to left, top to bottom in reading, for instance. "In the English newspaper," she continued, "they only put the important news in the centre of the paper and you have to read both ways—right to left and left to right." I think we should call editors the mediators between the West and the East!

I very seldom read in public, because I am afraid to find no space for my book. But I am very fond of reading in the British Museum for a time. When I get tired, after I have stretched my legs I look all round me at the other readers. Sometimes I can distinguish no heads in the row behind me, because they are all hidden in books. And sometimes I can only see a number of small reddish balls of flesh arranged in a row in front of me, because only the tops of the readers' bald heads are in sight. I wish I could be there more often to make sketches.

Another joy is to collect books. In China, nearly every family keeps some books in the house, as a sign of culture. Recently it has become a fashion for young Chinese not only to collect Chinese books, but also Western ones. In a modern house in China one will generally find Western and Chinese books mixed on the shelves. I do not know whether the owners have time to read all in their collection, but such a combination is certainly a sign of being not only a cultured person but actually one who knows a foreign language. If anyone of my fellow countrymen has the opportunity to go abroad, he generally brings quantities of books home in the language of the country where he has been. We in England are no exception. Not all of us may know London very well, but we certainly know where the book-shops are, especially second-hand book-shops. Foyles's and the shops around Charing Cross Road and, above all, the Caledonian Market are places where the Chinese are often to be seen. Sometimes the fee we pay for transporting them is more than we pay for the books themselves. I knew a friend who bought a large number of books at the market for about five shillings, so many that he had to hire a taxi to carry them home! From my own experience I can say many Chinese send case after case of English books to China every year. I think only Carter Paterson's Company can tell how many they have packed and transported up till now!

Hannen Swaffer has written a passage in the *Daily Herald* under the title "Ye Olde Bookes." He says:

"When the Antiquarian Booksellers' Association which has members in all the world's important cities, met for its annual dinner at the Café Monico, last night, it was grumbling. Business has fallen off; good copies of rare books are hard to find. The best specimens all went to America in the boom. . . ."

I hope the Second-hand Booksellers' Association, if any exists, would not grumble so much that the bad specimens all went to China in the boom! After all, simply to collect books is a great joy, and there is no need to buy the most expensive editions.

Mr. Swaffer has also written *Kleptomaniac*.

"In Charing Cross Road," he says, "London's book-selling centre, Sam Joseph tells me, dealers have regular clients who turn up every day at one, read the books in the boxes outside, and at two o'clock, before going back to work, turn down the corner of a page to mark it for the next day! They still tell the story of the old gentle-man with plenty of money and a passion for stealing rare copies. Every three weeks or so, he would do the rounds of the dealers' shops, "lifting" a book here and there.

They knew him, of course, and kept a check on the copies that disappeared. Regularly they sent the bill in to his secretary, who promptly paid. This suited everyone concerned, until somebody found out that one or two of the less honest dealers were sending in bills for books that he hadn't stolen, as well as for those he had. He's dead now."

It seems to me that the dealers are very kind to provide books for people to read without any payment. I have been one of their clients too sometimes, though not a regular one. I visit Zwemmer's most of all. It is funny to have this passion for stealing books. We have many people with that complaint in China, but we do not call them "thieves." We generally speak of them as "People who take books away at their own convenience." I have never heard of their being dunned by the owners, though it is annoying to have a book taken away by others. It is also true that people often borrow books and never want to return them. A friend of mine told me that Sir Walter Scott used to put a small card on the shelves of his library bearing words somewhat as follows: "Here should stand such-and-such books which have been borrowed by so-and-so on a certain day but not returned yet." Sometimes he would invite the friends to come and have a good look round his library without mentioning anything. I do not know whether it is true or not, but I doubt whether such a device would have much effect. In China we have considerable difficulties in refusing to lend books to others. How can we solve this problem? Better leave it to psychologists and lawyers.

There is a special custom in China I should describe here. We generally have scorching sunshine most of the time from July until the end of September. On the seventh day of the seventh month of every year every family *airs* their belongings, chiefly clothes and books, in order to keep them undamaged by insects. Girls are busy carrying out clothes, and boys books, for *airing* in the hot sun in our courtyards. When I was young I was always ordered to do this job. While I was airing them, I generally took some interesting books to read at the corner of a corridor, in order to amuse myself. It usually took several days for me to finish the job. It is said that there was a well-known scholar called Hao Lung, who lay down with the upper part of his

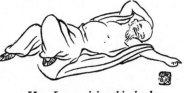

Hao Lung airing his books

body naked and his face to the sky, under the hot sunshine on that particular day. Then a friend of his dropped in to his courtyard and asked him the reason for this conduct. He answered that he was *airing* his books which were kept in his belly. This perhaps needs an explanation. In China, we read books and afterwards generally try to learn them by heart. A good scholar is said to be able to remember most of them from memory. So this one was very proud of himself remembering all that he studied, and was sarcastic at the expense of those who only aired real books. As soon as I was able to understand this story, I felt ashamed of my old job. I have not yet heard of anyone *airing* books in London!

幽園有鵝有荷花之枝鵝影
相摧磨白鵝一何肥花枝亦不
俗朝立花間游暮向花間宿
有時引吭作長鳴花亦鬧心助
顏色無端被風雨欺鵝亦
低頭鳴之泣情天自古無物別
羨汝居然同眷屬

Translation of the poem is on pages 20–21

About Statues

Possibly I have a little more time than most busy Londoners, for I can always manage to spare a minute or two to look at the statues in the streets whenever I pass them. At first I studied them for a good time, as such things are not to be seen in Chinese streets. Afterwards I grew accustomed to them and took much less notice. Now I begin to wonder whether Londoners look at them at all or ignore them completely. I go on asking myself: "Is London so small that I see statues everywhere always packed up closely round the buildings? Can anyone really judge a work of art carefully, in detail, if he is looking at it from a distance and suddenly a double-decker bus comes in between? Do the drivers and car-owners wish to have more space to drive over the roads? Why don't they let me find out what Nelson's face really looked like?" I cannot put down all my silly questions. One morning I was travelling on the top of a bus and while I was looking at the statues along Whitehall, a clear voice piped up from a small girl of four, asking: "Mummy, why do the people put up all the statues in the middle of the road?" The mother did not answer and I suppose she could not find a suitable reason for it. I wished I could reply for her. My own impression is that all those prominent people were in queues waiting to go into Parliament again, just as many Londoners stand waiting outside a theatre. Of course, it is a rather sparse queue just yet. But after another thousand years there will be plenty of statues, probably as many as for the first night of a play or a film!

133

Somehow I have a great affection for the Nelson Column. I like it particularly because of its height and prominence. Its site is well chosen too, and probably it is the most typical and unmistakable landmark of London next to the Houses of Parliament. Londoners may not think so but to a foreigner like myself, it gives this impression. We Chinese may visit many other famous places in London, but these two are the first to stand out. I remember about two years ago, a military friend of mine who has served in the Chinese army over twenty-five years, came to London on a European tour. He did not know any European language, so I had to be his guide here. He wanted to see the Houses of Parliament first, and we were obliged to pass Nelson's Column on our way from Hampstead. As soon as he saw it, he said to me that he liked it extremely. Then I took him round galleries, museums, palaces, Westminster Abbey, St. Paul's, the Tower, and so on, for about a week, but he always repeated that he liked this particular Column best. After he left, he wrote to me that except this, nothing had impressed him much in London.

Once Mr. W. W. Winkworth took me to a lecture given by Mr. Foster on *Ivory Tower* at 9, Great Newport Street. Before the lecture began we sat in the top room of the building, and he suddenly pointed out this statue from the distance through the window. It was standing far, far away, but it seemed to me that it stood over all—other statues were lost by comparison. I just think that it would be most impressive sight if there were only the Nelson Column in Trafalgar Square and only the Cenotaph along Whitehall, though naturally I have no right to criticise. I have heard a number of people say that the Cenotaph was beautiful, simple yet impressive, and others say it was just like part of a chimney or a water-barrel. But I think the sculptor was quite right not to make any design in bas-relief of the war front or soldiers killed on the battlefield to horrify the onlookers.

There are always gatherings or demonstrations taking place in Trafalgar Square and the bottom of Nelson's Column is used as a platform. Once someone said to me he wished there was no such platform ready for them there, and I suppose Cabinet Ministers feel a grudge against that platform too. By the side of the Column there is another feature I always notice—the flocks of pigeons. I wrote the following poem about them:

Scores of pigeons gather below Nelson's Column,
Sometimes flying there and sometimes here.
Being given some food, they will cluster together;
They will be happy if they are satisfied.
Alas! what is bread made of,
That it can have such power to defeat the flying capability of
  pigeons?

I may seem to have wandered a little from my topic, yet I always feel there is a great bond between pigeons and statues. Those statues which were erected without columns are generally very friendly to pigeons. Sometimes I have looked up and noticed something moving on the bald head of a statue. I thought first that the person was coming to life or something was amiss with him. But it was only a pigeon strutting about, proud of itself for standing on such a prominent place—the very top of an important monument! And those people sitting, standing or riding on their pedestals, perhaps drawing the attention of visitors for a little while, but always ignored by the eyes of ordinary passers-by, always the same year after year, must be very pleased to have the friendly pigeons jumping up on their laps, hands, shoulders, and heads to make a change for them. But I read in the newspaper one day about a certain place where a statue of a famous man was going to be erected and how this man declared he did not want his statue put up because he had no wish to provide a seat for pigeons. He is really very sensible, but when I think of the Society for the Prevention of Cruelty to Animals and Birds, I am afraid he might be summoned for lack of consideration to pigeons. It makes me wonder a little further whether the souls of the statues may not think their countrymen very cruel to them in exposing them to rain, wind, storm, fog, or even burning sunshine for ages without any shelter. Or their relatives or friends might feel uncomfortable as they can protect them-

Pigeons' seat

selves from rain or storm with an umbrella but the statues cannot? The following story was told in Shanghai some thirty years ago: A very wealthy and famous Chinese scholar, who had spent a lot of money in setting up a very good school in Shanghai, died. The trustees of the school then decided to put up a statue in memory of him, an idea which we had learned from the West. But his wife objected, because she did not want her husband to be standing under sun and rain all the time. She said that though she might not be seeing him like that all the time, yet she would not like to feel he was in that predicament. And the sons and daughters expressed themselves in the same way. So they came to an understanding by putting a bower over the statue. It is said the wife and children used to go up to the school and order the servants to wash and clean the face and all parts of the statue. From the Western point of view, this sort of performance might be considered very foolish or might be said to show that we are too sentimental or super-stitious. But I think one cannot help wanting to give a hand if one sees one's parent, children or very intimate friend with a dirty spot on the face which they cannot see them-selves. If one has known a person well, eaten, drunken, and slept with him through many years, after his death one can-not fail to be moved when touching an image exactly like him. I imagine one would be reminded of all the past inti-macies and probably consider it as alive. Confucius says: "You must consider God is there while you worship him." In the same way, one cannot help thinking the statue is alive if one loved the person very much. I think I would climb up and try to wash off the green particles, the white pigeon marks, or black dust, if I had been a good friend to anyone of the statues around Trafalgar Square and along Whitehall. Even though I have never known them as friends, I sometimes feel very uncomfortable when I see a well-known person whom I respect highly with a half-black and half-green face. I wonder why they are not put under shelter in a very good and artistic building.

As I have been in London for five years, the number of my English friends increases all the time. They are very kind to me and most of them talk with me very freely and frankly. I admire their point of view towards things and life in many ways, and especially that they show friendship with all types of mankind as well as with animals and birds, without bias and discrimination. One day I had a good talk with a friend on the subject of broad and narrow minds. We mentioned the main characteristics of most different nationalities in the world. I said I believed in the Confucian idea that every human being is born good but that he may be changed by circumstances into a different character. Then I remarked that I had found out a special feature of the English character from statues. My friend was astonished and immediately wanted to know what this was. I said that the English mind is very broad as a rule, but somehow there is some difference of degree in the breadth of it. I ventured to say that English people would not like George Washington very much, because he had separated America from England. But they wanted to show their generosity and give an impression of liking him, so they erected a statue to him. The point was obvious. They put his statue quite apart from others and made it rather smaller than the rest of them. That, I thought, was an indication that the English mind was not always broad enough. My friend burst into laughter and said that he had not seen this statue at all. I assured him that it was in a very unimportant position just at the left-hand corner of the National Gallery, so that I mistook it for a famous painter at first.

Talking about the English character, I always have the impression that it is very reserved, calm, and thoughtful. So I wonder how those great men can bear to stand in stone with noisy traffic all around them. I read somewhere that Gladstone was a very quiet person and preferred tranquillity to bustle, and Nurse Cavell was the same too. But they both stand in the noisiest possible places. I think Henry Irving was put in the right place, as he was accustomed to facing a huge audience.

In the *Observer* I once read:

"The statue of Charles II has been with due solemnity re-transported to the centre of London. This particular statue, though by no means a typical atrocity, does inevitably lead the mind to consider London statues in general and thus induces a vein of gentle melancholy. Why is it, one asks oneself, that the English, who are far from negligible in the plastic arts, should be content with bronze and leaden caricatures of their great men and women? Why is it, in particular, that horses so defeat the sculptor in the greatest horse-loving nation in the world? Watts, it is true, in 'Physical Energy' produced a steed that would have alarmed a dray-horse, and King Charles I's horse is a conventionalised royal supporter, but what of all the frozen lumps that carry generals and commanders wont to ride into battle at the head of a charging army? Do they symbolise the fact that it is the general's duty to be anchored behind the lines? Or are they an assertion that great soldiers, as being true democrats, prefer to be mounted on palfreys suitable to a jogging pilgrim? Or is it simply that we can't sculpt horses?"

I was very much attracted by this passage; firstly, because the writer showed he was interested in statues, as I am myself, and secondly for the information he gave me about the sculptured horses. Before the statue of Earl Haig was to be put up, I noticed there was much discussion over one of the horse's legs and its neck. After it was erected, I went to see it and tried to make some criticism of the leg and neck. But I must say that I could not find much difference there from other equestrian statues, nor do I see the sense in people paying so much attention at first and neglecting them entirely afterwards. I have been told that the mother or wife of the person whose statue is to be made often points out that the left ear or the small fringe of hair on the back part of the head is not exactly as in reality. Oh, I can imagine how much the sculptor must have suffered, even if his work had been specially selected. I always enjoy the imperfection in the perfection and silently appreciate the truth in the world.

Oh, fellow artists, try to be content yourselves with your own work and then you will have no worry.

There has always been a difference of opinion and much argument about Epstein's works every year since I have been here. Some admire them very much, but some condemn them entirely. An Academician has even resigned because of them. I do not claim to understand sculpture very much, so I can hardly give my opinion about Mr. Epstein's work. But I admire him for his bravery in working out a type of sculpture totally different from the conventional idea of "a likeness," and one which is, in fact, not a memorial but plastic art. I always think a great work of art will either give you a pleasurable sensation, or it will offend your eye very harshly. If it delights or maddens, then it is a real work of art which will stand for ever. I also like to look at Rodin's work now, although at one time it stabbed my eyes very sharply. Now I like to stand and look at it for as long as ever I can. If a sculpture is not used as a pure work of art, but as a memorial only, I would like to suggest that the Chinese way of remembering our ancestors and well-known personalities by making stone tablets with names carved in beautiful handwriting is a reasonable method, though I am not trying to make excuses for our sculptors, who are not in the habit of modelling the human form. Mr. P. D. Ouspensky, in his book *A New Model of the Universe*, has described his experience of looking at the Sphinx in Cairo as follows:

"But when I saw the Sphinx for myself, I felt something in it that I had never read and never heard of, something that at once placed it for me among the most enigmatic and at the same time fundamental problems of life and the world. . . . I remember sitting on the sand in front of the Sphinx—on the spot from which the second pyramid in the distance makes me an exact triangle behind the Sphinx—and trying to understand; to read its glance. . . . Its glance was fixed on something else. It was the glance of a being who thinks in centuries and millenniums. I did not exist and could not exist for it."

This is exactly how I think a statue should be!

奈爾遶前鴿子堆忽然齊飛

去又飛来投之以食則迴

集謀得一飽好懷開呶呶

麨色汝何物失郤飛揚跋

庵才

Translation of the poem is on page 135

A Study of Names

To me English names are interesting but puzzling. At first I was struck by the habit of calling different persons by the same Christian name. Passing along a busy street in London, I often hear people being called John or Charlie. In the parks, every second boy seems to answer to Tom or George. At parties, I soon noticed that many ladies were called Jean or Marjorie or Flora. I wondered how they distinguished themselves from each other, if three Johns and four Marjories happened to be together. Once I took part in a friendly conversation and heard a gentleman saying to a friend of mine: "Bill, don't you think this is all right?" "Yes, I think so, Bill," was the answer. I could not help asking my friend why they should address each other like that. He answered: "His name is Bill and mine is too." Then I said: "Don't you feel that you are addressing yourself?" "No, I've never thought of that," he replied. I am still mystified!

A Chinese girl came over here to study in a convent school. I suppose her Chinese name was difficult for the nuns to pronounce, so she was given the English name, "Margaret." But she told me that there were already three students called Margaret and so she was always wondering what was going to happen when this name was called. She found it very difficult at first, and then got to know the difference in the way the nuns called each of them. From her description it seemed a subtle distinction. However, she went on to say that she always looked up when this name was called and then looked at the nun's eyes. She was clever! I have frequently been told by my English friends that they know by instinct. They think my question is unnecessary, so I am still in a puzzle.

Once I read a letter from a lady in the newspaper, in which she said:

"I have recently named my baby daughter Mary Ann. I was aware that this name is out of fashion, and that it was regarded in the near past as somehow humorous; but I was unprepared to find it so unaccept-able to-day as it appears to many of my friends, who advise me to use an abbreviation. Other despised names have turned to favour. Why not Mary Ann?"

Presently another correspondent replied in the same paper and said:

"But there are other agencies at work besides fashion. Many names, like Oscar and Jabez, drop out from un-pleasant association. A good many disappeared through being used as subjects of ridicule in music-hall songs; and the War got a bad name for such terms as 'Cuthbert' and 'Clarence.' One never knows what accident may happen to a name to render it unpopular."

From these two passages, I am surprised and interested to learn that a name can be a despised or a favourite one. And an accident may also happen to it to render it un-popular. After all, it seems to me that we in China are certainly wiser on this point, for we choose our own names. It may happen occasionally that two people have the same name because we all pick out a name with a good meaning, but this is only one chance in a million.

I always imagine that English people must be delighted

if on reading a novel their name appears in it in such a good context as: "Andrew, you are so wonderful to have done it!" said by a beautiful girl; or, "Stella is the most charming girl I have ever seen," murmured by a handsome young man. But on the other hand, if a man named Henry saw a heading in the evening paper: "Henry— charged with manslaughter," would he read about it?

I have another explanation to offer why English people like to be called by the same names. I suppose they consider that all men are brothers, so they like to address each other by the most popular names they know. Sometimes I have been addressed by some drunkard as "Jack" or "John" when I looked in at some public bar! Besides, kings, queens, princes, and princesses all have the same sort of names as the people, and this is a further sign of the English democratic nature.

I think that in China the choice of our names has undergone a sort of purification from early times. A Chinese book says:

"There are five different ways of choosing names; but we cannot choose one from the name of a country, from an official title, from the names of mountains and rivers, from the terms of secret diseases, from the names of animals and from the names of money."

But in the second century B.C. even names from these categories were used occasionally. If we go far back, there were persons called by their birthdays and by the number of persons in the generation, and also a lot of people took their names from their occupation. They had very peculiar names too, such as "Black-Kidney," "Black-arm," Sheep's Back," "Fox-Hair," and so forth. After a time these were abolished and names for men became most frequently associated with Confucian virtues and those for girls with flowers. But we only have one hundred family names, though we can have as many first names as people care to select. It is funny for me to see that English people can choose only from a limited number of first names, but they can have as many different family names as they like. I am not in a position to discuss their origin or how they changed, but I must say I had a very amusing time going through the London telephone directory from the first name to the last for three whole days! I know people like to hear and know of other people doing stupid things, though they do not like to do them themselves! I found there many English family names which were beyond my imagination. For instance, a very charming girl with beautiful lips may belong to a family called "Campbell," which generally means "disproportionate mouth." A handsome young man belongs to the family of "Cameron," which means "twisted nose." A thief may be called Mr. Noble; a sick man walking very slowly is called Mr. Rush; a dwarf may have the family name "Longfellow"; a member of Parliament is Mr. Butler. Oh, there are too many for me to think of! I can imagine that no lady likes to be born into a family called "Old" or even "Older." Surely no one can help being miserable if he is always called Mr. Poor or Mr. Farthing. It would be interesting to know what the host or hostess would think if one of his or her guests was called "Greedy." I wonder how people address those who have such family names as "Younghusband," "Darling," "Love," "Dear," and so forth when they become intimate friends? A Mr. or Miss Loveless may have many lovers and a Monk is perhaps not a monk! I do not think I should have the courage to speak to a Miss Dare, Miss Male, Mrs. Manly, Lady Marshall, or Madam Strong. Suppose there is a heading in the newspaper: "Miss Middlemiss Missing," I shall be puzzled whether to interpret middlemiss as a middle-sized or middle-aged person if Missing is a family name. You may argue with me that any proper name always has a capital letter at the beginning, but I am afraid that some of my fellow-countrymen who are just beginning to learn English will complain that a sentence such as "English's car runs over" has a grammatical mistake in it, if they do not know that "English" stands for a person's family name. They will never understand the meaning of sentences like "England reaches England" or "London is in London." We generally play games with each other's names, and I suppose it is the same in England, and probably the games will be even more amusing. We very seldom play with family names, because they provide little variety, but in English it will be the other way round. I have tried to work out a short story using only English family names helped by a few prepositions and conjunctions. And I have composed it in the Chinese manner without change in the verb for the third person, without articles, and very seldom using a pronoun. It runs:

Coward Man and *Dark Child*, not *Goodchild*, *Call Fisherman* and *Buy Fish*. *Fisherman Handover Herring* to *Child* and *Coward Man Fry Herring* from *Gray* to *Brown*. *Wise Fox Take Herring* for *Child Making Full Joy* with *Coward Man*. *Coward Man Walk Down* with *Knife* and *Child Call Loud* that *Man Want* to *Man-Slaughter Child*. *Whatmore?*

All words in italics are the family names. Once I came across a Cumberland farmer whose name was Lamb. He and a friend of mine were good friends, so they addressed each other by the family name only. As we three sat together, they began talking absorbedly about lamb. My friend said: "Lamb, how is the lamb?" and went on to mention the word frequently in their talk. I must confess that I did not follow the conversation very well!

The harm of blood marriage was known in our early history. Hence persons of the same surname or family name were not allowed to inter-marry since the twelfth century B.C. Even though our surnames are limited to one hundred, we have never had the case of a couple both having the same family name. A young man from the North will never think of making love to a girl who has the same surname as his, even if she lives in the South. It is interesting to know that English people can marry someone with the same family name, though they have such a vast number of names. For instance, in a paper it says:

"It is announced to-day that Miss Joan Macneill Campbell, elder daughter of Sir George and Lady Campbell, of Pyrford, Surrey, and Calcutta, has been married in Calcutta to Mr. Kenneth Macrae Campbell, younger son of Mr. and Mrs. J. Campbell, of Harrow."

The journalist seemed to be interested, as he added the heading: "Married—kept same name." I do not know whether there is really any harm in this kind of inter-marriage, but we Chinese seem to think that same names descend from the same ancestor. I do not think we shall ever change this idea, even in the present march of time! The Chinese is the most conservative race in the world!

There is another difference between English and Chinese names. According to English ways, the Christian name stands first and then comes the family name, but with us it is just the reverse. Since I have been here, I have frequently been called Mr. Yee, but actually I am Mr. Chiang. Some people have been very cautious and addressed me as Mr. Chiang Yee!

Many London street names are also extremely interesting. I would like to quote here some from the "New London Street Dictionary" in *Punch*:

Air Street—Doctors send their patients to this locality for change.

Amwell Street—Always healthy.

Coldbath Square—Very bracing.

Distaff Lane—Full of spinsters.

Fashion Street—Magnificent sight in the height of the season.

First Street—Of immense antiquity.

Friday Street—Great jealousy felt by all the other days of the week.

Great Smith Street—Which of the Smiths is this?

Idol Lane—Where are the missionaries?

Love Lane—What sort of love? The "love of the turtle?"

Paradise Street and *Peerless Street*—Difficult to choose between the two.

World's End Passage—Finis.

These certainly grow in interest from the interpreter's definition of them! Though many street names in London are those of Christian saints as well as of kings, princes, and well-known families, yet I do not know why there are several roads called "London Road," as if they were in some other foreign city. I like to think there are places called "Snow Fields" and "Half Moon Street" because I can so rarely see snow or moon in London. Once I went to Rotten Row, but nothing was rotten there; another time I was in Patience Road and could see only people dashing impatiently to and fro. There are two more places in London that have stuck in my memory. They are Meeting House Lane and Makepeace Avenue. I wonder why those people who enjoy meeting and peace conferences do not come over here!

巍々國會古建築一時
獨步西方雄任汝古界
萬變化我有成算羅
心胸會場神態比天
氣慨在濃雲薄霧中

詠英國之會

Translation of the poem is on page 65

At Galleries

First I must congratulate Londoners on their luck—they have easy access to handsome art collections, and this is a pleasure we have not enjoyed in China until recent years. Before the revolution most of our works of art were kept in the palace, and none could see them except a few high officials. There were, besides, some good private collections which were never shown to the public. Unless we were rich enough to collect ourselves, we rarely set eyes on a masterpiece.

Our artists, too, believe they reveal their inmost feelings in a painting, and for that very reason are unwilling for the crowd to gaze on it, and smirch it with lack of understanding. It is only recently this attitude has changed and we have begun to build museums and public galleries. I hope we shall be able to show the highest perfection of our art, equal to the world's masterpieces, if we pass through this crucial time.

I must record here my first experience of an English art gallery. This was the Whitechapel Gallery, which was showing an exhibition of Chinese paintings. When I had seen everything and was preparing to leave, I felt both reluctant and curious. There in a corner sat a young man looking at a painting most seriously and meditatively. He was sitting there when I entered and he had been sitting there all the time. At last he came up and spoke to me, and on learning I was a painter, immediately became more interested. He led me to a table in the centre of the room and brought out the photograph of a Chinese landscape.

He said he owned the original. Then he got out from another pocket a small album with about ten pictures in it. After that a framed painting appeared—though I have no idea where it came from—and finally two little Chinese drawings. I was more and more astonished with each

emergence, but I suppose this is the great advantage of Western clothes with their prodigious number of pockets! He invited me to his house to look over all his collection, and I discovered that this strange young man lived in a very fashionable quarter of London, in a fine old building with lovely objects surrounding him, and that his father was a well-known collector of Chinese porcelain. Since that day we have become good friends, and though we have had all kinds of larks together, we may not correspond for a year on end. I value his opinion on art in general very highly. He gave me a joyful first experience of London galleries, and I think we shall keep friendship for ever. Who is he? He is Mr. W. W. Winkworth, whom I've spoken of already.

At Whitechapel Gallery

After this I started visiting the National and Tate Galleries. I usually chose to go on student days, because there were fewer visitors, and I had many an interesting chat with the art students who came there to copy various masterpieces. I was astonished to see some of them attempting to copy huge, detailed paintings, with ladders to examine the top parts, and rulers in their hands. This was quite a new light to me on Western technique. Standing before a painting called *Derby Day* by William Powell

Frith, I amused myself picking out the face of each figure in the copy and comparing it with the original, while the artist was away. They were exactly alike, dot for dot, stroke for stroke, colour for colour, and shape for shape. When the copyist—a lady—returned, she appeared very pleased that I should be studying her work so seriously, but she did not know that all sorts of strange ideas were passing through my mind. She told me with pride that she had been working on that painting for about six years, and that only half was finished yet; it would take at least six more years to complete. Then she pointed out which figures she had taken most pains with, and which had turned out exactly right, and told me finally that she wished to sell the finished copy for five hundred pounds. I held my breath and listened to her story with astonishment and attention, but could not express a single word of appreciation. After thanking her and moving away, I decided I could no longer call myself a patient person!

I used to accompany Professor Ju Péon, a Chinese artist, while he was copying one of Raphael's Seven Cartoons in the Victoria and Albert Museum. After helping him to unpack his instruments and materials, I would stroll round to look at the exhibits, and perhaps have a chat with some of the wardens. I once asked one of them whether he enjoyed this kind of job, whether he ever looked at the paintings, or whether he knew them all by heart. He just laughed and said, "Oh yes, sir, I do look at them occasionally; I have to remember them all very well, you know, because the visitors make all sorts of inquiries. There's plenty of amusement here. When I'm tired of standing, I have a chair to sit on in the corner. I take a nap now and then. Afterwards I can stretch my legs and walk up and down. You'd soon find out what a lot of fun I had i you took on my job, sir!" We had a hearty laugh, and I could not help admiring his good humour.

I really enjoy some of the smaller galleries best, and the Leicester Gallery is one of my favourites. I shall always remember my impression of Epstein's exhibition there a few years ago, when *Behold the Man* was on view. The little room where the statue stood was packed with people; I noticed two groups standing in the corners trying to get a better view. On the faces of the first I saw smiles that seemed to say that this was a work of genius, beyond the reach of comment. But the smiles on the second group expressed something like derision, "What a monstrous figure!" It is strange that a smile on a baby's face is always the expression of happiness and pleasure, but when a grown person smiles, he may express mockery, cynicism, or pretence. How crooked a man's mind becomes as his experience widens!

Visiting the Exhibition of Modern French Art at New Burlington Galleries again on the last day, I found the rooms crowded out with fashionable visitors, and as the time for closing approached, so more and more poured in. It was hardly possible to look at the paintings, so I began to study the people instead. It certainly seemed to be a society function, smart young ladies were crying "Hallo!" and "Hallo!" in all directions, shaking hands with acquaintances and making small talk. I heard a girlish voice raised above the general hum: "My dear, we've been so busy these days, we simply couldn't get here a minute earlier. It's lovely, isn't it? The pictures are *too* charming, aren't they? . . ." Then the time was up, and the exhibition closed. This disrespectful way of approaching art is quite beyond my oriental mind!

Not long ago, Mr. A. W. Bahr and I were dining together at Young's Chinese restaurant in Wardour Street.

Just as we were finishing, Mr. Bahr noticed Mr. Augustus John and some of his friends going out, and hailed them. "I say, John, where have you been all this time; I've not seen you for ages!" "Oh, I've not been out for three years," replied Mr. John, with his two big brilliant eyes glaring. To me, his powerful glance had some relation with the extreme strength of his brush-strokes. A friend once told me that Mr. John's nurse had dropped him on a stone when he was a baby, and knocked his head, and that from this accident his genius developed. I daresay there are plenty of artists nowadays who wish their nurses had been as careless! In China we have a lot of stories like that—how such-and-such a person was struck on the head or startled out of his wits by the sight of a dragon, so that he instantly became a man of genius. Another type of story is about a well-known scholar who dreamed that an ancient sage presented him with a beautifully coloured brush. After he awoke he was suddenly able to write miraculously good essays, and from that day began his reputation as a scholar. Unfortunately, some years later, the sage came into his dream again and asked for the brush back. From that night his style degenerated!

To my surprise, many people have asked whether I have any interest in Western paintings, and have been rather incredulous when I protest that I enjoy studying them. To be sure, I have gained a great deal by going to look at Western masterpieces from time to time. I think a highly developed craftsmanship in experimenting with light and shade and colour is undoubtedly the gift of Western painters. I also admire the variety of composition they achieve. For instance, one painting of a mother and child may look the same as another to a Chinese at a superficial glance, just as dozens of Chinese landscapes look similar to the Westerner, but in fact, there is much more variety

156

PLATE X. *Mr. Laurence Binyon*
(IN MR. LAURENCE BINYON'S COLLECTION)

in Western figure painting than in our composition of mountains and streams.

I cannot enter into art theories here in much detail, but I should like to quote a few sentences from one of my lectures; I said there:

"I believe the whole art world may be divided into followers of Apollo and Dionysus; Apollonian art represents strong feeling, deep thoughts, and powerful manifestation of affection; Dionysian art is quieter, more peaceful, shows an affection which is reserved, but tenacious and lasting. I also believe these two types may be taken to represent the respective arts of West and East."

Again I said:

"Chinese artistic technique is subjective and etherial, putting human feeling into harmony with the spirit of Nature. The art of the West by contrast I may call objective and dramatic—it uses human power to control Nature. Out of these characteristics of the West arise realism and the idealising of the human figure. The Western artist likes to control, as it were, this human form—to give all his sculptured figures the grace, strength, and perfection of an Apollo or a Venus. He tries, on the whole, to catch the light exactly as he sees it in life, and the colours as they strike his eyes. This is the basis of the difference between Western and Eastern art, for in the East we do not care about symmetry of form or reasoned order. . . . While trying to put a spirit into Nature's forms, we accept the appearance of those forms just as they are without idealising them. . . ."

On the whole, I find my reaction to every type of Western

painting is one of movement—quite the opposite of the feeling inspired by my native art. I think Western artists reflect the outlook of this side of the world—man as a vigorous, adventurous being—whereas we Chinese consider ourselves so small by comparison with the universe and the long history of mankind, that even if a tiny figure in a Chinese landscape is painted in action, it does not affect the general tranquil atmosphere of the huge mountain and long river. The tree leaves may be moving in the wind and the water rippling, yet they show no disturbing, restless force. But in a Western landscape, the laws of perspective reduce the distant mountain to a small hill, and trees or figures in the foreground become the main feature of the work, and any kind of movement in them is impressed at once on the onlooker.

I like the works of Constable and Turner immensely, but almost all of them give me a feeling of powerful and drastic movement. On the other hand, the two works *Cremorne Lights* and *The Fire Wheel* by Whistler make me feel more as if I were looking at a Chinese painting. *The Avenue* by Hobbema has the same effect, and Corot's works particularly attract me by the tranquillity of their colouring. I must say too that I find a very interesting treatment of water in the Italian room of the National Gallery, very similar to one of our Chinese styles. Four or five scenes of Venice have wrinkled lines on a background of dark blue colour, to show the surface movement of the water, and this is exactly our technique!

Besides my interest in the composition of Western paintings, I always like to look at the brushwork. I was first recommended to look at the works of Burne-Jones, and for quite some time I liked them, but tired of them at last. Though his composition is rightly celebrated, I do not find his brushwork at all striking. Sargent's brushwork is extremely skilful, but I have the feeling that his strokes stand apart from the canvas, and are not sticking to it. His brushwork is striking to the eye, in the same way as Burne-Jones's compositions, but neither bears looking at continually. I can never forget Holbein's portrait of *Christina of Denmark, daughter of Christian II of Denmark,* in the little room, and the works by Rembrandt and Hals. *The Shrimp Girl* of Hogarth, the portrait of *Dona Isabel Cobos de Porcel* by Goya, and the *Agony in the Garden* by El Greco also hold me spell-bound each time I am in the National Gallery. As I said in the chapter "About Statues," a true work of art if it does not give you a pleasurable sensation, will offend your eye harshly. I think the works of El Greco especially always give me proof of my belief.

We Chinese always wonder why Western artists are so fond of painting the human figure—especially the female figure—in the nude. Dr. Lin Yutang once pointed out that when a Westerner thought of "Victory," "Liberty," "Peace," and "Justice" he instinctively imagined a woman's naked body, and Dr. Lin wondered why that should be. The history of the introduction of nude painting into China is worth recording. On their return from studying Western art abroad, some students held an exhibition in Shanghai, including many studies from the nude. A storm arose at once in the Press. It was said that the minds of the whole nation would be polluted. Some of the older generation who had been brought up on Confucian ethics demanded that the government should ban the exhibition. The first artist to use a girl model in an art school, Professor Liu Hai-Su, was put under warrant of arrest for some years! For many years there has been conflict on this question: the old stagers said that the sight of a woman's naked body would excite young minds and lead to immoral action, but the modern artists declared that the beauty of the curved lines in a woman's form was the most important thing in art. The conflict is growing a little less severe nowadays. Even in the West there have been controversies on this point, and I was told that when the *Venus and Cupid* of Velasquez was first hung in the National Gallery, an English lady took a knife and scratched it in several places: the scratches are still to be seen!

I want also to say something about portrait painting, which is the main sphere of most Western artists. I think more than seventy per cent of the works in London galleries are portraits. But this type of art does not hold a high position in China, because we think the artist will have to twist his talent to follow the sitter's mood. My father was a portrait painter, though he liked to paint birds and flowers more than anything. He confessed to me that he could hardly refuse to paint a portrait, as he was well known in that branch of art, but he was not very willing to do it as it meant giving up his freedom for a time.

It may be interesting to Westerners to know that we do not paint portraits from a few sittings; the artist must go and live in the sitter's home for some time in order to catch his different moods and true personality. Our painting never relies on light and shade; accurate and significant lines play the important parts in portraits. There is an amusing story told of one of the Ch'ing dynasty emperors who rejected a portrait of himself by a Western artist because, to his disgust, the artist had apparently made half of his face black, and purposely added a big smudge under the nose!

The more familiar I become with English water-colours, the more points of similarity I find between them and our paintings. The treatment in the black-and-white wash drawings of Cotman, Cozens, Constable, and Cameron, make me believe there is really no boundary between English and Chinese art at all. Once Mr. A. P. Oppé was kind enough to ask me to dine with him and to show me his lovely collection of drawings by Cotman and Cozens. Among them was a tiger by Cozens. Mr. Oppé told me that the artist had dabbed several spots of wash on the paper, and had found a tiger taking shape before his eyes. This is just the Chinese way of making a painting. During my five years in London I have made many friends through mutual interest in Chinese art, and I greatly hope that in the near future we shall be able to provide facilities for studying it, so that people may realise that art knows no narrow national or racial boundaries.

不知花氣是衣香
消得荷風幾許涼
攬碎一湖明月影
飛來三十六鴛鴦

沙本塘湖客独主

Translation of the poem is on page 74.

On Plays and Films

Though I do not go to the theatre often, I am very much interested in the queues standing outside London booking-offices. They are a typical sight in London, and one we never see in China. They are a cheerful crowd—extraordinarily merry, unusually patient, and remarkably strong in the legs! An American friend told me there were no queues in her country either, except occasionally for the opera. I can well understand that, for I doubt whether any American has time to stand still for a couple of hours on end.

One of my countrymen has cultivated the queue habit to a remarkable degree. He has a perfect passion for plays, and is an economical person as well. The first row of the pit is as fine as a seat in the stalls, he says, and two hours' waiting will save him nine shillings. He says he can sit happily on his stool at the head of the queue and study his books every bit as well as in the British Museum. He is a lucky man! I think the people in the pit are perhaps the real audience for the play.

But I cannot well understand why theatre managers prefer to keep people standing outside rather than let them occupy those higher-priced seats which are, in fact, often empty. And I admire the queuers for never grumbling, but only expressing the hope that there will still be room for them.

The first play I saw in London was *On the Rocks*, by G. B. Shaw, and it was being produced at the Winter Garden. The theatre was not full, though, to be sure, the

164

PLATE XI. *G. B. S. in trouble*

play had only been running about a week. But I had imagined anything written by so famous a playwright would draw huge audiences. Perhaps it had not enough entertainment value for the general public. It is strange how everything Shaw writes brings us back to thinking of the man himself. I saw in *Punch* a design for a statue of "John Bull's other Playwright," with two figures in it—one a huge G. B. S. and the other a small Shakespeare. Both were pointing to a sign on which were written the words, "Man and Superman." After reading *The Adventures of the Black Girl in Her Search for God*, a cartoon drawing suggested itself to me in which G. B. S. was being seized by the black girl who was crying, "I have found my God!" to which he replied, "No, my dear, you are wrong, I am not G O D, but G. B. S."

I have never seen him in person, but his twinkling deep-set eyes always amuse me when I see him in a film. I don't think he likes the sun! He has spent a short time in China, and I thought he might bring back some impressions of the young Chinese playwrights and the modern girls who fêted him in Shanghai. But in this play *On the Rocks* he only mentioned that "the Chinese calls us Pinks." A true observation!

Some time later I saw John Gielgud's production of *The School for Scandal*, and I must confess I like this classical type of play better than many of the modern ones. Dr. M. T. Z. Tyau says:

> "If, therefore, the Chinese stage is to a Westerner too much make-believe, the Western stage is to a Chinese over-realistic. After all, we go to a theatre not to see real life, since there is already in actual life too much pathos and drama, but to see only a portrayal of life."

Probably there will be differences of opinion on this point, but I must also confess I have no relish in seeing on the stage the life I can so well realise outside it. But I thoroughly enjoy a realistic portrayal of the life in Shakespeare's time and at various periods of past history. I love the Western stage settings and the design of the costumes in such plays; I think they help wonderfully to recreate the life of the period, and they often have intrinsic artistic value. We might well adopt this idea for our own stage.

But I do not think special settings or costumes are necessary to these plays of modern society life. I saw *Antony and Anna*—a play which ran successfully for nearly two years in the West End. My friend asked me what I thought of it, and I could only reply that the actors and actresses might simply have walked on to the stage after their morning's shopping in Oxford Street or Bond Street! Another play, *Love from a Stranger*, also made a curious impression on me. First of all I could hardly believe that such a charming modern young lady could possibly fall in love with a stranger after the first conversation—and a stranger who did not smile once during the whole play. It was a tense drama, but the face of the leading actor did not convince me that he could win a lady's heart. Now Vosper is dead, and the riddle of his death has faded already from the public mind!

I go to the Palladium occasionally to see the variety shows. My most vivid impression is of Gracie Fields singing Lancashire songs. Though I could not understand the dialect, I found the greatest pleasure in her voice and gestures. In China too we love to have some well-known person sing local songs with native gestures. I think the joy of listening to this sort of thing cannot be easily analysed into words; it is something to be felt and experienced.

Perhaps it would be in order for me to say something

here about our own theatres and plays, but I do not think I
need make a lengthy explanation after the production of Mr.
S. I. Hsiung's *Lady Precious Stream*.   I think anyone who has
seen this play and compared it with *Chu Chin Chow* will not
be in any doubt over their relative merits, but I should like
to describe some of the difficulties Mr. Hsiung had to
overcome before the play appeared.   He certainly showed
patience and determination.   For a whole
year he tried to find a manager to take
it, and I think it was rejected eleven
times, and among those who refused to
take the risk were Sir Barry Jackson and
Mr. Leon M. Lion.   It is interesting to
note that after *Lady Precious Stream* had
become a popular success, Mr. Lion himself played the part of the prime minister
for some time, and Sir Barry Jackson took
the play to the Malvern Festival!

Lady Precious
Stream

   Messrs. Rieu and White of Methuen's
are really to be praised for their discrimination, for they published the play in book
form prior to its production, and so, since it
had had very many favourable reviews, Miss Nancy Price
agreed to take it on after the strong persuasions of Mr.
Jonathan Field.   The next trouble was to find costumes
from among English collections.   Some of them varied in
period as widely as a thousand years.   Finally Mr. Hsiung
had to attend rehearsals faithfully for four weeks, every day
from morning till evening.   Not every playwright is troubled
in this way, but in a play where the whole dramatic tradition was strange to the actors and actresses, there was no
help for it.   An actress might want to wear a man's embroidered robe, or an actor would insist on donning a lady's
skirt.   The foreign princess found it very difficult to learn

our way of riding on horseback, and wanted to scamper about, using the whip like a rope. And the prime minister insisted on pulling off his beard from time to time because he declared it chafed his upper lip, and none of them wanted to take it very seriously, and they often joked among themselves—"Are we really going to wear these clothes on the stage?" Mr. Hsiung's good humour over everything is much to be admired and his success well deserved.

Armlet of Jade was once produced at the Westminster Theatre, but owing to difficulties of production again it did not enjoy a very long run. But the play—a popular story from the Chinese Golden Age—was excellently written, and I very much hope it can be produced again some time and give the general public a vivid idea of our theatre and life.

What is better known to every Londoner than a rare Chinese play is the Russian Ballet season at Covent Garden Opera House. I was taken there for the first time by Sir Alexander W. Lawrence and the two young Lawrences, John and George. I enjoyed the classical ballet *Fire Bird* particularly, though I know nothing about dancing or Western music. Then came the modern one. In it there was a male dancer with two long bunches of whiskers attached at both ends of his mouth, and another bunch in the middle of his chin, wearing a costume partly Japanese and partly perhaps Chinese and holding a small painted parasol which, I presume, Japanese ladies may carry. While he was dancing in peculiar contortions, the small parasol vibrated and the three long bunches of whiskers quivered in opposite directions, so that I could not stop my laughter. John suddenly said to me that that was how most Europeans imagined the Chinese. I thanked him in my mind for not having used the word "Chinaman"! I nodded my head and continued the conversation: "It is very interesting to me, because I have never seen things like this before. Should we actually dress and behave like that, perhaps it would not be so laughable." Luckily I managed not to blush when the interval came and many curious eyes turned towards me. In another book, *Chinese Calligraphy*, I said:

> "During the three years I have spent in England, I have heard a good deal of the Russian Ballet, and have myself seen several of its performances. The kind of pleasure I personally derived from watching it closely resembled, I found, the aesthetic emotion involved in calligraphy. After some experience of writing one begins to feel a movement springing to life under the brush which is, as it were, spontaneous. . . . The sensation is really very like that aroused by a ballerina balancing upon one toe, revolving, leaping, and poising on the other toe. She has to possess perfect control of her movements and amazing suppleness. The same qualities are demanded of the writer. A dancer's movements follow the rhythm of the accompanying music: a writer's movements depend upon the length and shape of stroke of the style he is practising, which may thus be said to correspond to the music."

This is a reason special to myself for liking Russian Ballet.

I have also seen Indian Ballet performed by the Uday Shan Kahr company. Though the atmosphere and flavour were completely different from the Russian, the joy I experienced was of the same nature. I was particularly fascinated by the movements of hands and fingers.

I have seen many films in the past five years, but perhaps

I should confine myself here to my impression of *The Good Earth*. The novel was already popular, and the description of our peasant life in the northern part of China in that particular period so good that the film was bound to have a success. I saw it three times myself, and though I think the studies of the two chief characters were rather exaggerated, the film has certainly increased the understanding and sympathy of English people towards the Chinese. One of my friends told me of a wonderful remark she overheard as she was coming out of the cinema: two factory girls were chatting together, and one of them exclaimed in surprise, "They're not really Chinese—they're human beings!" Thank heavens and Mrs. Pearl Buck for turning us into human beings!

泰晤斯河叶色青落芎吹漾碧

波明一竿漠翁笑在手垂釣閒

垂柳楸陰古人太怳翁太閒仰

看白雲自往還魚忽奮鬐作人

言怪爾釣者何柯熟水面船艇

布如織機聲軋軋不安全载來

避地此枘空部又遣汝釣者欺

嗚呼天地到處皆殺機

Translation of the poem is on page 104

About Teatime

Had I not come to London, I should never have known there was a special time for tea. Tea-drinking has become the customary adjunct to meeting people or having a rest or refreshing oneself, and seems to be a human habit indispensable to most of the English race. I have heard many jokes about it, even that during the Great War, a division of English troops was commanded to storm a town in enemy hands about four or five o'clock in the afternoon, but none of them would follow the order until they had had tea. Dr. M. T. Z. Tyau says:

"Just as the Frenchman is often of an excitable nature, because of his coffee or absinth, or the German is dull and heavy because of his beer, so the English is of a quieter disposition because of his cup which cheers but does not inebriate. . . . Therefore the Englishman is serious and almost ascetic, whereas the Frenchman or German is light-headed as well as light-hearted."

I cannot form a general idea of the Frenchman or German in my mind yet, but I certainly agree that English people are very serious indeed!

Are they ascetic? This is a debatable point, I think. Once I attended a tea-party of a character unusual to me. There were about twenty people present, and we sat around a long table together. I was put between two elderly ladies. As we were passing the teapot from one to another, I thought I ought to be polite, so I offered to

pour the tea for the lady who sat at my right-hand side.
I had also learned to ask her whether she would take milk
and sugar, and she answered "Yes." But I poured milk
in first and then the tea. The lady suddenly noticed what
I was doing and hastened to say with warning finger raised,
"tea first!" She insisted on my changing the cup. I was
very surprised and asked myself why she should be so
particular; however, I obeyed her order! Later, a young
Chinese lady told me that she was thankful not to be an
English hostess, because she would have to remember how
many pieces of sugar her husband liked to have in his tea,
and also the number of pieces of sugar for each of her
husband's friends. If she poured the tea or coffee out, she
must ask first whether they liked it weak or strong, white
or black. It seemed to her that all this was not worth while
bothering about, but she was surprised to know that most
English girls were very fond of looking after such things.
Anyway, these intricacies give the hostess some occupation
during her tea-parties.

The word "tea" is said to be derived from the Fukienese
pronunciation *ta*, and "that excellent, and by all physicians
approved, China Drink, called by the Chineans *Tcha*, by
other nations *Tay* alias *Tee*," was advertised for sale three
centuries ago (in the *Weekeley Newes*, 31 January, 1606)
at the Sultaness Head, a coffee house in Sweetings Rents,
near the Royal Exchange, London.[1] And it was also said
that tea was first introduced into Europe towards the close
of the sixteenth century by the Dutch. It seems to me that
most of the countries in Europe all began to drink our tea
at that time, but why did it only become a pronounced
habit in England? Is it due to the specialities of English
weather or to the English character? And what was the
Englishman's daily drink at four or five in the afternoon

[1] Williams : *Outlines of Chinese Symbolism and Art Motives.*

174

before the end of the sixteenth century? Actually tea began to be used as a national beverage in China only in the T'ang period (A.D. 618–905). I have not found any record yet of what we drank before that time. Since we have begun to drink it, many of our forefathers became great tea-lovers and a large number of books written on this subject have been published, discussing the treatment of tea-plants, their kinds and the places where they grow in China, and especially dealing with the art of making

Gathering dew from lotus leaves for making tea

tea and how to enjoy drinking it. I am afraid I have not room to tell all about it here, but I would like to point out one fact. During that early period, our Imperial government found that it was a good means of raising money, as everybody took up the tea habit. So they imposed a heavy tax on it and introduced numerous regulations to prohibit smuggling. At the beginning of the eleventh century, in the Sung period, the tax became even worse, and there was a common whisper going round the whole empire at that time, that "Tea is a tiger" because it had caused a lot of distress to the people. I wonder whether I dare point out that the British Chancellor of the Exchequer has considered making some increase in the tea-tax before he announces his budget every year. This has happened every time during my five years' stay. I hope I shall not find myself in prison for writing this!

Although tea has fallen hard on the taxpayer, yet we love to drink it constantly. We have no regular time for it; we drink it when we like, and not merely for refreshment:

it is a form of sociability, a unifying element whenever friends may meet. To our tea-lovers the making and drinking of tea is an art as well. We always serve our guests with a cup of tea when they call at the house, either formally or informally. I think this is sensible, because the friend is very grateful for refreshment after a long journey, or may need to be warmed up if he comes in wet and cold weather. As well as tea-lover asking tea-lover to come for the special enjoyment of tea, no one in China is expected to call on anybody without being served with a cup of it. As this is so, it has another function. Sometimes one has to receive a visitor whom one does not know well, perhaps only by introduction. Tea is served as usual, but we do not drink it at once. Then the man begins to explain why he is paying the call. If the host is interested in the matter, the talk will go on and both will sip tea at intervals: if not, the host will purposely say "Shall we have tea?" which is another way of telling the caller he ought to go. As we cannot be so impolite as to send the person away directly, this action serves by mutual understanding as a token for ending a conversation. But this is only a custom performed among strangers or new acquaintances. Unfortunately, some strangers simply ignore the custom and just go on talking, especially when they are applying for a job, even if the host has indicated his lack of interest.

Anyway, tea-drinking in company is not a bad custom; good friendships often begin that way. After we really become intimate, we abandon any such idea of dismissing a guest, and generally a better quality of tea is served. We have many different kinds of tea and some of us can easily distinguish them at the first sip. We prefer to drink tea very fresh, so we pour the boiling water into the cup itself after some tea-leaves have been put in it first. Sometimes we enjoy looking at the leaves and never pour them away even if a second cup is needed. Of course, we have another way of making tea in a good teapot as well. But we very seldom have cup after cup, because we do not gulp them down. Our best kind of tea is a clear, pale golden colour, which is quite different from what is sold in the London cafés and restaurants, and certainly not like Ceylon tea. Nor do we need any milk or sugar to flavour it; we think the natural flavour and scent of the leaves should reach our palate in their original purity, and so we sip it appreciatively, little by little instead of cup by cup, as I said in *The Chinese Eye*.

In London, I have never been served with a cup of tea when I called on an English friend, unless it happened to be at teatime. As a rule, I never call on anybody here unless I have made an appointment beforehand, and generally I always meet friends at this special teatime. I know it is a good idea to arrange one's plans ahead, but somehow I feel I have an objection to it. I prefer to do things naturally, that is to say, quite without much formality. Apart from business matters, I think people might meet each other in a freer way, at their own convenience. Perhaps English people do so among themselves—I do not know. As I am a foreigner here, I feel uncomfortable in asking anybody to meet me at very short notice, even though I consider him a very intimate friend of mine and think he may be in the mood for talking with me. When I feel in the mood to talk and discuss I dare not ask a friend to come, and by the time a few days have passed my mood for that special talk or discussion has completely vanished, and our meeting becomes formal and forced. Oh, how difficult human life is! And how complicated at the present day! I can imagine that some of my readers will very much disapprove of what I am saying about making arrangements with friends, but needless to say, I always think of things by putting myself in the other's position. For instance, I know people are always busy, as I myself generally have something to do. However, I think we might live a little more naturally, like the animals or the birds. There is a Chinese friend of mine who has been living here over twenty years. As he is much older than me, I pay him very high respect and always follow his advice. Once I asked him to come down to my place for a meal and we had a very joyful time together. But he instructed me in fatherly fashion that I should not make arrangements at very short notice, pointing out that I had written to him only two days before. He said English people would never accept this kind of invitation. As he is likely to be right, I obey his words. Another time, I was told by an English friend that the people would think themselves unwanted guests and be unlikely to accept the invitation if they were asked only a day or two beforehand. What more can I say about it? Only that I prefer to be alone! Sometimes I find it very hard to be alone in London; not because I am not able to remain alone, but because people seem unwilling to allow me to be so. And I am afraid I have lost a few friends in England through being so reluctant to mix in social circles and attend innumerable tea-parties.

There seem to be few other ways for us Chinese to make friends except by attending such parties. Any of us who come to London are generally taken to tea-parties by the old-stagers for the first few months. At first we are interested in the custom, but after a time we try to get rid of these recurrent obligations. I think I could make a very thin pamphlet with no more than twenty popular sentences in English, which are generally used by English people at teatime. Anyone of us who does not know English at all, could manage very well to attend tea-parties for years and

PLATE XII. *Rhododendron's time in St. James's Park*

years if he learnt those sentences by heart and no more.
I suppose most people know what they are!

At teatime, the host or hostess seems to be occupied all
the time pouring out the tea, making sure whether the milk
is to come first or if there is to be no milk, and asking how
many lumps of sugar people take. Then they pass round
cakes and again pour out second cups and perhaps a
third round. By this time people are getting ready to
leave. Once or twice I thought it strange not to have said
one or two complete English sentences to them at all. It
simply seems to me that teatime is a special form of
business hour. The host and hostess consider themselves
as business managers making arrangements for their
clients. As soon as their clients are satisfied with a cup or
two, the whole business is over.

"In ordinary cases the English afternoon tea is a
most enjoyable function," Dr. Tyau said, "but at times
the experience is far from comfortable. I refer to par-
taking of afternoon tea in a lady's 'At Home' party.
The function takes place in the drawing-room, where
everybody is supposed to put on his or her best behaviour
and, in the case of a lady guest, also her best hat and
gown. You have no table where you can put your cup
and saucer, etc., but all the paraphernalia must be
securely perched on your knees. As soon as there is no
one to disturb you, you are tolerably safe. You balance
your cup and saucer in one hand, and use the other to
act as the connecting rod between the delicacies on the
plate, which is resting on your knees, and the cup of tea
which is to wash them down. But you are neither free
nor easy."

I could not understand this when I first read it. But

after some experience I began to wish I could be a great deal fatter in order to have a wide lap to hold things safely. But it will never be an easy performance, for as soon as everything is adjusted I have to get up to greet a new guest who comes into the room. If it is a lady guest, I have to yield my seat to her. Sometimes I have found no seats provided, and all the guests standing shoulder to shoulder. Then I am always puzzled as to whether I should do without the cup of tea for safety. And often I could not get it at all because there is no room to reach the table. I always find it a trouble to get another piece of cake or sweet, so I generally leave a small part of the first one on the plate to show I have not finished. Again, some hostesses are always keeping watch on their guests with sparkling eyes to see whether one has someone to talk to or not, but they sometimes drag me away from my first acquaintance when I am just beginning to know his or her name and introduce me to another. Once I was in a very awkward position, having been led away from an interesting conversation with a friend of mine and introduced to a young lady leaning on the mantelpiece in a beautiful afternoon tea-frock. She just nodded her head and said "How do you do?" when I was introduced. Then she did not say another word, but just went on leaning on the mantelpiece and I did not know myself what to say. After sometime, she took out a cigarette from a box which was quite near her. I do not smoke, so I kept no matches. I felt acutely embarassed. Then she asked for a match and pointed to the near-by table. As I was beginning to move, another gentleman turned round, and offering her his lighter, began a conversation with her. I was thankful to be released and enjoyed my silence until the end of the party. Probably it is this sort of situation which keeps me away from tea-parties!

As tea is an important factor in English life, there is no small alley without one or two places for tea in London. Of course there are also many fancy ways of taking tea in the good hotels, and therefore a great business of making cakes. "Home-made" is the typical English recommendation. Apparently English girls have at least one important business to learn—how to make cakes. It seems to me that everyone can make one or two kinds, but I'm afraid they all taste the same to me. When we have tea in China, we simply enjoy the tea itself. The following quotation may give a poetic idea of Chinese tea-drinking:

After lunch—one short nap:
On waking up—two cups of tea.
Raising my head, I see the sun's light
Once again slanting to the south-west.
Those who are happy regret the shortness of the day;
Those who are sad tire of the year's sloth.
But those whose hearts are devoid of joy or sadness
Just go on living, regardless of "short" or "long."[1]

[1] By Po Chu-I (A.D. 772–846). Translated by Arthur Waley.

胸中塊壘總難平

誰挽銀河洗甲兵

天亦如人多變化

時晴時雨不分明

雨中有感

Translation of the poem is on page 91

On Food

Food is a daily topic in London. As it is essential to life, it is certainly a subject on which I have much to say, particularly as I was not brought up to eat the same food in the same way as Londoners. We have something to eat in the early morning, but it is not the same as London breakfast. I think to have breakfast in bed is quite unknown to us and I really do not know how one can eat in bed. When I have been kindly asked to stay with friends I have always wanted to take breakfast downstairs after getting up. But sometimes I have felt I should make the host and hostess feel awkward if they did not get up to keep me company, so I generally prefer to have a cup of tea and some bread and a boiled egg in my room. I always get up beforehand. Although many people speak of "eternal" bacon and "hard-as-bullet" eggs, yet I like them. Sometimes one or two small fried herrings are as good as anything else, but I am no friend of sausages of any kind. After salty things, toast with butter and marmalade, not jam, is my favourite. Or I may just have the latter alone. I regret to say that I can hardly eat porridge, though it is a common first course. Sometimes I have tried to swallow it with the help of sugar and milk, yet it is hard to finish the whole dish. Once a German boy told me that he got tired of porridge, porridge, and porridge every morning in his boarding-school, and I shook hands with him on the spot.

English breakfast is certainly a good beginning to the day, but it takes a little time to enjoy it properly. When

I joined a party going to Brussels, I read a warning notice in the programme which said something like this: "It is strange that on the Continent they do not serve good breakfasts such as we have in England. One must not complain about it as it is their custom." It is strange for me to see how English people emphasise this breakfast. But I also wonder if the people who come here from the Continent are warned about English bacon and eggs?

After their hearty breakfast most Londoners, I am told, do not take much at luncheon. But what they call the light midday meal seems to me only shortened by taking off the soup and dessert perhaps. Afternoon tea makes up for the light lunch. And at last a solid dinner finishes the day until the next breakfast. These are the usual English meals every day. But I know one may have morning tea before breakfast, or morning coffee between breakfast and lunch, or a supper after dinner! How many times they eat I really do not know. And even then, some people suffer from *night starvation*! What a wonderful new invention, and how clever are the Western doctors! Such a thing has never been heard of nor imagined by us. It is stranger still that those who suffer from *night starvation* are women, not men! Most Londoners always complain of lack of time, but I think they have plenty of it, and that they perhaps spend too much on eating and drinking. Half an hour for breakfast, an hour for lunch, three-quarters for tea or a little more for high tea, an hour and a half for dinner, half an hour for a drink, and an hour for supper. If attending a sherry party is included, and all the time spent in getting to meals, I doubt whether Londoners ever stop thinking of food all day long. In addition, I do not know how much time women spend drinking Horlick's milk in order to prevent *night starvation*.

People are always complaining about English food, even

English people themselves. It is interesting for me to see some of the better restaurants in London giving their menu in French. When I have been there by myself or have been taken by friends, I could not order the dishes because I know no French, but to my surprise some waitresses or waiters did not read them properly either. The dish itself seems hardly different from what I have had in other places, so I begin to wonder why they print the menu in that way? "English cookery is plainsong," says M. André Simon, "American cookery is jazz, French cookery is classical." "Jazz" is perhaps not suitable to the English temperament and "classical" may be a little too high a standard, so why not "plainsong"? I myself rather like English cooking, because it is mild and clear. Though the dish may not be very highly flavoured, yet there is something both for taste and nourishment. I read an interesting passage by Mr. Randolph Churchill in the *Evening Standard* the other day:

"The English and the Americans probably take less interest," says he, "in their food and know less about food than any other race in the world. The women, if possible, take less interest than the men. Not content with being uninterested themselves, they are very apt to regard any interest they may detect in others as sure signs of greed or ill-breeding. Conventionally minded folk have come to accept this taboo and food is held to be an unsuitable and almost improper topic for conversation, particularly at the table. The result of this conspiracy of silence is that the art of cooking is held in low esteem throughout the Anglo–Saxon world, and the English-speaking people, both in their homes and in their public eating-houses, are condemned by their own laziness and inhibitions to the dullest and worst-cooked food in the world."

Ah, this is quite opposite to my impression here.
think any English person can talk on food as well as th
French. From my own experience, though they ar
generous and modest enough to say that they like Frencl
food, yet they very seldom admit that English food is no
good. Sometimes passing by a shop which sells foodstuf
or when buying food myself, I notice that anything Englisl
is dearer. And I remember having dinner once with thre
elderly English friends in Holborn Restaurant. On th
table were English and French mustards. One of then
said that he ought to be patriotic, but he preferred to hav
French mustard. And the second said that Englisl
mustard was always best of all. Then the third wondered
why it was the fashion to like French mustard. In my turn
I had to join in, and uttered: "I never take mustard, s
I can't tell." As a result I was praised for my diplomacy
If a condiment like mustard can form a topic of con
versation, the talk about real food must be more extensiv
than one can imagine. I think within the last two year
English people have talked about food more than usual
but in a different way. Since the Minister for Co-ordina
tion of Defence has urged this country to grow more food
to ensure the maintenance of efficient supplies in time o
war, I have been able to find the word "food" in th
papers every day. Now, just think of war, food, and th
art of cooking! I am bound to think of refugees too.

It is true that one cannot expect to get a nice dish i
the food is produced in mass. Therefore dishes served in
restaurants are generally in this plight. Though there may
be many good restaurants in London, yet they lack per
sonal care such as can be given at home. Owing t
business concerns and the speed of public life in this bi{
city, it is a natural tendency for people to have their mea
in a public eating-house. Besides, in the restaurant ther

is always a lively scene and some places entertain the visitors with comedians and musicians, which I think is the most effective method of diverting the visitors' attention from the taste of the food. I doubt whether the cooks really know much about what they are cooking if each kind of food is prepared in a great quantity. Anyway I think they are all good psychologists to keep the customers waiting until any food tastes superb. I also think it is clever of English cooks just to fry, boil, bake, or roast the stuff and leave salt, sauce, and pepper on the table for the consumer to apply for himself. A Chinese cook would cut the meat into small pieces and see to the proper seasoning of the food as well. Probably the English cook thinks the eaters can cut the food big or small as they like. I must say that I sometimes find it difficult to cut the meat off the bone of a chop and as I like it very much I have to give up the attempt with my mouth watering.

It is very difficult for me to say which dish I like best among English foods. Before I came over here, I had trouble with food because I could not eat strong-smelling things, and very seldom took beef or mutton. For one reason mutton or a lamb chop seems to me always to have a smell which I cannot endure, and as for beef, it is not the kind of meat I was brought up to take. There is a general belief in China that ox and cow have done so much good to mankind, ploughing the field for us to grow rice and other foods, that we should not kill them. I remember my grandmother used to tell me when I was young that Occidentals were very unkind to the ox and cow, as the latter gave them enough milk to drink every day and yet they still wanted to eat her! As my grandmother was the head of the family, we did not have beef for meals. This is only a family custom, and one which makes me feel uncomfortable when I am confronted with

beef, but many of my compatriots are very fond of it.
Since I have been here for a long time I realise beef is the
principal English meat, and as I have to take it on many
occasions I begin to make friends with it more easily now.
I like roast beef, the English national dish, and Yorkshire
pudding. As I was told that Simpson's and the Café
Royal were both famous for their roast beef, I went to
those places to eat it occasionally. I prefer it to be a little
more than *middling done* and not *under done*, which horrifies
me. And I cannot take it cold. Stewed mutton is still an
obstacle for me. I like all kinds of fish except sardines.
Steamed cod or fried herring suits me well. Once when I
was invited to attend the annual dinner of the Fell and
Rock Climbing Club of the English Lake District, real
Cumberland ham brought down to London from its native
place made such an impression on me that I still remember
it. We Chinese are fond of meat, chiefly pork, but we do
not take meat alone for a dish; it is always chopped into
very small pieces and cooked with all sorts of vegetables.
So our cook can use one kind of meat to make many
different dishes by mixing it with different kinds of vegetables. We have the belief that meat makes people fat.
I wonder why most Londoners always hate to become fat
but never give up taking big slice after big slice of meat
for meals?

England does not grow a great variety of vegetables, and
the few kinds there are are one and all called "greens."
Greens are the most regrettable part of an English meal to
me. I do not mind so much not having many kinds of
vegetables, but the English way of cooking vegetables is
very unacceptable. Those such as spinach, cabbage,
cauliflower, broccoli, and potato are generally over-boiled
until they have lost all flavour. I wonder who can tell
me what is the exact taste of mashed potato and exactly

what they feel when they have it in their mouth. The last part—sweet or pudding—after the main course of every meal is generally delicious. But I cannot take raw celery nor cheese owing to their smell. I have never tasted Chinese cheese in China, so I have not dared yet to take English cheese. Sometimes people have tried to persuade me to take a little by telling me it had no strong smell, but I was never convinced. When I stayed at Parkgate for a fortnight, I was served with the famous Cheshire cheese at every meal, but I did not take it once. One day I received an invitation to a dinner at Ye Old Cheshire Cheese, of Fleet Street. I hesitated for a long time, because I feared that cheese would be the main dish. In China some restaurants specialise in a certain dish and they use it for their shop sign. I supposed it was the same here. I went, however, in the end, and fortunately I had a very good dinner without having to touch cheese. I had a curious feeling towards this place, because it looked much like some old restaurants in China's big cities. Though the arrangement of the furniture and the drawings on the walls are quite different, yet the atmosphere is more or less · the same. In old restaurants we feel entirely at peace, drinking, eating, chatting, laughing, or recalling stories of some distinguished person in art or literature, or some beautiful ladies of historical romances. There is no thought of time, whether old or modern, early or late, and no care of whether we talk of heaven or earth, east or west; this is how some of us spend the whole afternoon or evening at those old restaurants. And certainly we do not allow any business talk on these occasions. The waiters might tell us of this or that prince and nobleman who had been to the place in the past dynasties, but I do not think they would hang up or bother to preserve many relics of them. In Ye Olde Cheshire Cheese there are many historical associations, as I learned from the talk at the dinner. It was rebuilt in 1667 after the fire of London and has existed since then. I like the following story I read of an old waiter:

"William Simpson commenced as waiter in 1829. Old 'William,' for many years the head-waiter, could only be seen in his real glory on Pudding Days. He used to consider it his duty to go round the tables insisting that the guests should have second or third, ay, and with wonder be it spoken, fourth helpings. 'Any gentleman say pudden?' was his constant query; and his habit was not broken when a crusty customer growled: 'No *gentleman* says pudden'."

It is interesting for me to imagine the crusty customer, and enjoy the flavour of the local dialect on the word "pudden." I dare say customers who come to this place would always like to taste one of the features "Ye Toasted Cheese," but not me!

Charles Dickens and Dr. Samuel Johnson were both customers of this restaurant. In Dr. Johnson's dictionary there is a sarcastic definition of pie: "any crust with something in it." I think this is true, because I can never tell what is in an English pie though there are many kinds. I do not know how an English pie is made, but I think M. Boulestin might be wrong when he said: "An English cook throws away more food in a week than a French one would in months." I do not think an English cook throws away much, otherwise there would not be so many pies. Anyhow, a Chinese cook would never throw away anything, for he can keep the bits to make "Chop Suey." If M. Boulestin was right in saying that the test of a good cook is soup, I think the Chinese order of courses might be acceptable. The soup is always served first in London, but in China we generally take it at the end of the meal, and so we can look forward to it longer. If good soup comes first and not very good courses follow, one will be disappointed; but it is still possible to hope if the order is reversed! We really could not have a meal without soup, even if the other courses may not be appetising, all will be appeased by a good soup. I have learned to cook some Chinese dishes for myself sometimes, though I cannot say I know cooking. And I am amused to find that some of my English friends cook their food in the same amateur way as I do. When allowed to be present in their kitchens, I have watched them busily peeling potatoes or mushrooms, turning page after page of the cookery book, and reading the time indicator as well. Some of them keep a glass cylinder engraved with the measurement of the volume of water in use. I am reminded of experiments in the chemistry laboratory in my college days! A Chinese friend once cooked a breakfast for me entirely in the English fashion. I wanted to turn off the gas when the egg had been boiling for some time, but he suddenly stopped me and said that it had not boiled four-and-a-half minutes yet!

The English system of serving one dish after the other is certainly a more elaborate and hygienic way than ours. This idea we should adopt, and I think some of us have tried to do so already. As a rule, when we have a meal, we sit round a table and all the different kinds of dishes are placed in the middle of it at once. Each of us is provided with a small bowl of rice, a pair of chopsticks and a spoon. Therefore our chopsticks and spoons have sometimes to meet in the same dish. But now a clean pair of chopsticks and a spoon are generally laid in the middle of the table for serving, so we need not put our own chopsticks and spoons in the common dishes.

I have heard that most English people think that we Chinese eat much more than they do, because they know a Chinese formal dinner or banquet generally has twenty or thirty different courses. Perhaps they think we finish them all, but I must say that I do not touch a number of them when present on such an occasion. When one talks about Chinese food, one is bound to think of the names, "dragon's liver" and "phoenix marrow," as well as "bird's nest" and "shark's fin" and perhaps even "cat's flesh" and "dog's flesh." I have heard of the last two quite often in China, but, so far, I have never seen anyone eat them. There is a Chinese parable which runs as follows:

"There lived a man who became notorious as a living fount of obnoxious smell, the intensity of which was such that none of his relatives or friends could bear his presence. Tormented by this enforced isolation he took refuge at the seaside, where, as it happened, he met someone who was lured into following him night and day by that very smell which had driven him from home."[1]

This makes me think that anything is possible in the universe. Some French people might be very fond of snails and frogs, and a few Chinese might eat cat's and dog's meat. But they should not give a reputation to the whole people.

When I first arrived here I was deeply impressed by a family dinner. There were seven of us altogether at the table and I was put on the right-hand side of the hostess. As soon as we all sat down, a manservant carried in a huge dish and placed it in front of the hostess. She lifted the cover and disclosed the complete leg of a pig. My

[1] Translated by Dr. K. T. Sen.

breath was taken away for a little while, because I did not know what would happen next. Then the hostess stood up in a triumphant manner to preside over the joint. I suppose you can imagine what she looked like if I say she was the type of lady in Rubens's paintings. English ladies' evening dress has no sleeves to be rolled up out of the way, so for preliminary she rubbed her hands together. Afterwards she took an enormous knife in one hand and a long steel in the other. After sawing for a little while, she changed the steel for a big fork and began to cut the leg into small slices. If I had been still a small boy of ten or so I should have been screaming by that time, because in my house we would never allow the appearance of any kind of knife except in the kitchen—and then for some special use, when it would be kept in an unnoticed place. And some Chinese ladies, for instance my sister and cousins, would simply tremble all the time and might drop it if they were asked to hold a large-sized knife. I had a good many curious thoughts at that dinner, but I could hardly describe them. One question which I have not yet solved is why she should start with such an appearance of much to-do and end merely by cutting off a thin slice of the meat for each of us. It seemed to me that she did not carry out the promise of her big task at all! I do not know whether we had this practice in the very ancient times of our history or not, but now we certainly do not bother to cut the food ourselves but have it ready prepared by the cook, and we eat with chopsticks instead of knife and fork. Ku Hung-Ming says: "Western civilisation is a knife-and-fork one, but Chinese one of chopsticks." I can hardly say that he is right to choose these examples for interpreting the Western and Chinese civilisations, but chopsticks have given some help to our scholars and philosophers. One of them writes:

I often wish to consult my chopsticks,
Which always taste what is bitter and what is sweet before
we do.
But they answer that all good savour comes from the dishes
themselves,
And that all that they do is to come and to go.[1]

There is another interesting story about chopsticks which a Chinese student told an old American gentleman. It is said that this old gentle-man was very interested in things Chinese, but he had not met a Chinese before. When he was walking in the street he met this student. He began to talk to him and they became friends afterwards, so he asked the student to dinner at his house one day. While dining, he asked some questions about the Chinese way of eating. "I know," said he, "Chinese do not use a knife and fork, but chopsticks. You put all the dishes in the centre of the table and the people sit around it. What would you do if you had a great number of guests? And what size is the table?"

Co-operation and mutual help

But the student did not think very carefully, and as he was studying mathe-matics answered that the table would be in direct propor-tion to the number of the people. The old man became puzzled, and said again: "How could your chopsticks

[1] Translated by Dr. M. T. Z. Tyau.

manage to reach the dishes?" Then the student, being at a loss, tried to support his own words and said, "The length of the chopsticks would be in the same proportion. We do not help ourselves, we always help others sitting opposite to us. This is called co-operation and mutual help." I do not know how the talk continued. In any case we like to think of chopsticks whenever we eat. "A greedy, gobbling guest said to a neighbour at a dinner-party, 'You don't seem to give your chopsticks much exercise.' 'And you,' retorted the other, 'don't seem to give yours any rest'."[1] I do not think this would happen at an English dinner table!

This reminds me of Mr. E. Bolton saying that: "Boys should be educated in the art of eating." But from my impression, the English manner of eating is admirable. I have never seen anyone being gluttonous over his food, and people always exercise self-control, in eating too much as well as too little. Somehow I have the feeling that they are at their business when eating too, the procedure for serving is so complicated. Changing plates, knives, forks, and spoons keeps the waiters busy, and passing the salt, pepper, and sauce bottles gives the eaters very little time to think of the taste of the food. Although English people generally make no noise while they are eating, I like to listen to the clinking of the knives, forks, and plates as they strike each other, making a kind of musical rhythm.

I was once thoroughly startled by the toast-master at a Grosvenor House dinner, who was dressed in a fine red uniform and held a wooden rod which he struck on the door three times, just as I was mingling with the guests. As soon as we finished our courses, I jumped again when he struck the rod another three times and announced that we had the chairman's permission to smoke. I do not

[1] Translated by Prof. Giles.

smoke, but I was very interested to know that a chairman, really in the sense of host, could give orders for smoking to his guests, which seemed quite contradictory to ordinary social etiquette. Shortly the announcer struck the rod again and then the after-dinner speeches began. These were very amusing and well done by some, but they became dull and long, as one followed another. I watched an old gentleman sitting opposite me who yawned once for the second speaker, twice for the third one, three times for the fourth one, and so on. At last he did not yawn but faintly snored!

海月不易得，得此
彌可貴。月下發高
吟，清光耀肝肺。四
顧絕人蹤，得披�@
足閣

觀月　區@

Translation of the poem is on page 73

On Drink or Wine

I hesitate to write the title of this chapter, having been told that England produces no wine, that all her wines are imported, and ruinously expensive as a consequence. If there is no wine here, why write about it? And as I hardly drink at all anyway, how could I write about it even if I wished? But this is a topsy-turvy world, and it seems to me that the higher the price of wine, the more it is drunk, and while I can never drink much, still two or three small glasses of sherry will be enough to make me break silence and tell some stories about wine in China.

In my experience, the typical Londoner can take his liquor with the best, and is always willing to "have another short one." Whenever I hear the query "Have a drink?" a hearty answer is sure to follow: "You bet!" "Rather!" "I don't mind if I do!" Most of my Scottish friends are proud to tell me, "We come from the land of whisky" or "We have many good ales, especially Younger's." But the Irish would say, "Guinness is best!"

The number and variety of foreign wines amaze me, and I am even fascinated by the different forms and shapes of wine glasses. Brandy is one of the names that comes to my mind first, and I have two happy impressions of brandy-drinking that I shall never forget. The first time was at Parcevall Hall in Yorkshire, where my host, Sir William Milner, produced a bottle one hundred years old. I can see now the expression of one of his guests, Mr. Marcus H. Smith, who sat opposite me. He curled his fingers caressingly round the glass, sunk his nose in it, closed his eyes, and smelt the fragrance for a long time. Then he tilted his head back, and with eyes still closed slowly savoured each sip, emitting sounds like "Heng" and "Hai" and long sighs of satisfaction. For a few minutes he spoke no word, then he opened his eyes and murmured, "You just smell it. Sip a little of it and taste it." I was quite lost in appreciation of his unspeakable enjoyment of the drink. I suppose anyone who has had the same experience can easily understand what I am trying to describe.

The second occasion was at Mr. A. W. Bahr's house. After the usual table wine had been drunk, some special large-bowled glasses were produced, into which was reverently poured just enough of some fine old brandy to cover the bottom. I saw Dr. Le May, former British Consul-General in the capital of Siam, bury his nose in the glass, and with closed eyes appear to hold his breath for a long time. He did not speak even a word after he put it down empty. His quiet manner and graceful movements added to my impression of his pleasure. Presently he told us that Siamese monks approved of English gentlemen very highly: "Once I visited a temple in Siam," he said, "and a grand old monk there told me he thought the quiet, slow way in which English people took their food reminded him of their own and the Buddhists' manner at table." I am sure if brandy were allowed, the monks would be even more expert in the graceful management of their glasses!

Though I am no drinker, I like to slip into the public bars occasionally to have a look at the merry side of London life. Wine is an enchantment to smooth away the sad part of life, and I think I must cultivate the taste soon! I usually try to stroll in by myself, for then there is less likelihood of the occupants noticing me, and I can study them without their studying me. I often drop into the little pub near my digs, and begin to find many familiar faces there. Some of them have a passion for dart playing, and as I watch them laughing and joking over their game, I forget the existence of sorrow for the time being. I once saw a merry fellow who had drunk more than enough trying to pick up a dart from the floor, but he no sooner got hold of it than he dropped it again, time after time, and with every attempt he laughed the more. His good humour was boundless, though I am sure in his sober moments his own clumsiness would have maddened him. He reminded me of our great poet and drinker, Tao Yuan-Ming, who used to play a stringless musical instrument after he had drunk wine. Let me quote the following passage from Dr. Lin Yutang:

"His only weakness was a fondness for wine. Living very much to himself, he seldom saw guests, but whenever there was wine, he would sit down with the company, even though he might not be acquainted with the host. At other times, when he was the host himself and got drunk first, he would say to his guests, 'I am drunk and thinking of sleep; you can all go.' He had a stringed instrument, the *Ch'in*, without any strings left. It was an ancient instrument that could be played only in an extremely slow manner and only in a state of perfect mental calm. After a feast, or when feeling in a musical mood, he would express his musical feelings by fondling and fingering this stringless instrument. 'I appreciate the flavour of music; what need have I for the sounds from the strings?' "

I dare say my Londoner would say that he simply appreciated the dropping and picking up of his dart, and did not need to score a bull's eye!

I have seen many women in the bar too, which of

course is contrary to our Chinese custom. I was interested
to learn that London policemen dislike dealing with in-
toxicated women, because they are apt to fight and scratch,
while both public opinion and their own sense of courtesy
prevent them from hitting back. I once saw a tipsy lady
in the Tube: she smiled at everybody, laughed, sang, and
tried to make conversation with all her neighbours.
Everyone in the compartment was laughing too, at her
remarks and expressions. It is no easy thing to make a
crowd laugh, and many experienced comedians have
failed at it. Wine is an enchantment!

I have read various stories in the newspapers about in-
toxicated people, and some of them entertained me highly.
Here is one of them:

> "Emerald Brady, of Portersville, to save the police
> trouble, arrested himself, lodged himself in the city
> prison, and signed a complaint charging himself with
> intoxication. The next morning Judge E. E. Ridgway
> ruled that Brady should work on the city chain gang to
> earn his bed and board, which had been provided in the
> prison after his self-arrest."

I think it doubtful that Brady was a good drinker! Another
story is about a less ingenious drunkard:

> "After having broken into a house, a native burglar
> opened the liquor cabinet and mixed a cocktail in a
> large jug to the following formula: one and a half
> bottles of whisky, one bottle of sherry, one bottle of
> stout, two bottles of soda-water, and a quarter-bottle of
> methylated spirits. He then cooked food in the kitchen
> and sat down to enjoy a convivial meal with himself
> in the lounge. When the owner of the house returned
> the jug was empty and the burglar was under the table."

The reporter pointed out that "a cocktail experiment proved to be the professional downfall of this native burglar," but at least the burglar had a very fine drink first!

Though I am not much of a drinker, I had many amusing experiences in China. It is the custom with us at a dinner or a banquet, that the host or hostess must press the guests to eat and drink, and it is almost impolite to refuse. I became thoroughly tipsy for the first time when I was dining at a friend's house in Nanking. The young girl whom I wrote of in the moon chapter was making a flower painting when I arrived, and after she had finished I added a few rocks for the background. Then we had dinner together, and to put an end to my protests against drinking, she and her sister held my head, pinched my nose so that I had to open my mouth, and so forced me to swallow three small cups of Chinese yellow wine in succession. It was a torture to me, but the whole household laughed heartily at my predicament. I really cannot describe the scene which followed, but they have never let me forget the wild things I talked about in my tipsiness!

When I was in the Civil Service at Kiukiang, some of the English ships used to call there, and the officers and I exchanged visits. I was once invited to dinner on the *Bee*. I could speak very little English then, and brought my secretary with me. After I had been shown round the ship, I was immediately offered a drink, which I now know must have been sherry. I knew my own capacity, but thought I could manage one or two glasses of it, and imagined I had to make the attempt out of politeness. At dinner I had to drink again—two glasses of another sort. In the lounge afterwards more bottles were produced, of different coloured wines, and the sight of them made me tremble! How could I excuse myself? The rear-admiral began explaining to me that the red meant "courage," green "safety," blue "peace" and so on, and insisted on my sampling them. With some trepidation I ventured on the blue. As I left the ship I felt my head growing very large and my body swaying, but I managed to get home somehow!

Listening to the sound of the River

Some days later I invited these same officers to a Chinese feast in my garden. They seemed to enjoy the food and drink, and especially appreciated the Chinese yellow wine. I soon reached my capacity, but they were encouraging me to "Come on," as the servants filled their cups over and over again. Being the host, it was my duty to keep them company. But one of my servants had the good sense to fill up my cup with red Chinese tea, so both parties were satisfied! After dinner we strolled about the garden and drank still more; the last thing I remember was that we all had our arms round each others necks, and were talking together in the friendliest possible way. But I did not understand a single word they said! There were about twenty of us, and we finished thirty-six bottles between us! I had even better fun with the American naval officers when their ships called at Kiukiang, for at that time they were still under "Prohibition"!

In conclusion, though I could tell a string of stories about well-known Chinese drinkers, I shall quote only part of a poem by Su Tung-P'o:

To-night I drank at East Slope—sobered once, drunk again.
On my return it seems to be the third watch;
My boy-servant already snoring loud,
No one answers my knocking.
Leaning upon my stick, I listen to the sound of the River.[1]

I am afraid some English wives might push their heads out of the window and shout, "George, why are you so late?"

[1] Translated by Ch'u Ta-Kao.

愛平森林好顏色入
秋更作十分豔唱出
東方異影來漫步
林間踏紅葉

秋林獨步　啞

Translation of the poem is on the bottom of page 34

On Men

I can never refrain from having a good look at London's typical menfolk whenever I meet them. I use the word "typical" here to mean genuine Londoners as opposed to foreigners who have lived in London for a long time. When I first arrived at Dover, I was asked by the customs officer whether I had any of the articles printed on a board he held. The officer seemed to realise that I could not understand English well and mentioned the articles to me one by one, as if he had learned their names by heart. I always answered "No," but told him that I had a watch, which I took out from my waistcoat pocket and showed him. After I had opened my case, he did not even trouble to examine the contents but just marked it with the chalk and let me go. Being grateful to him, I wondered to myself whether this is called "the system of honesty." My thoughts turned to the story of "a country of gentlemen" in a well-known Chinese novel, where, it is said, everything is done in unimaginably gentlemanly fashion. For instance, a buyer comes to a shop and wants to buy something. He praises the goods for being beautifully made and of good quality, but the shopkeeper answers always in the negative. He then persists in his praise and offers a high price for some object, but the shopkeeper refuses to accept it and asks him to reduce the offer lower and lower; he cannot sell him such bad goods at so high a figure. In that story all kinds of manners in society conform to an ideal standard, but one rarely to be met with in real life. However, at that moment in Dover I thought the customs officer was conducting himself in the manner of the "country of gentlemen"! Once a friend of mine came over here from Paris to spend the day, so he did not bring even a small suitcase. At Dover, after he had assured the customs official that he had not brought anything with him, the latter kept asking him whether he had this or that article as if he was reciting a passage of an essay. Then my friend flung his two arms wide, to which the officer could only smile and say "Thank you." My friend could not understand such queer conduct, but I told him that was "English." The officer asked him about dutiable articles, because he was a dutiful servant!

The London policeman appeals to me more than anything else in my life here. Probably most Londoners have cause to think of him sometime, but I myself have a special connection with him. As I am taller than most Chinese here, my fellow-countrymen always nickname me "policeman" whenever I go among them. Inspired by this, I used to approach the admirable London "Bobby" for comparison. But I always withdrew again hastily as soon as I came up close—he would be towering above me. On many occasions I go out with Mr. S. I. Hsiung, the playwright, who is rather short, and he always warns me to beware of his hat falling off when he looks up to ask the policeman something! Somehow I feel all London policemen are brothers and twins, because they are the same height, talk with the same expression and walk in the same manner. Though their faces may not be the same, they have the same immovable expression and when they smile, they very seldom let me see their teeth. I dare say there is no one who does not feel rushed in the London streets, but those policemen are unusually dignified and sedate in their walk. I wonder where most of them learned their mathematics, for whenever I ask my way, they

generally answer a "three-minute," "five-minute" or "ten-minute" walk from where they stand. Actually it is always double or three times their estimate. If I tried to walk at their speed, I should always be too late for my engagement. Once I complained to a friend about this, but he said that probably the policeman did not want to discourage me!

The policemen take part in any kind of public meeting or demonstration in London, but they never show any sign on their face when people joke about them openly. I have proved this every time I have listened to the public speakers in Hyde Park. I had a special experience on Jubilee night, three years ago. It was a national holiday and the gayest night in the life of every Londoner. I did not try to see the procession, but I watched very silently what was going on from Trafalgar Square to Buckingham Palace all night long. Cars drove up but could not get through, and the people in the cars turned out to join the street dancing. Presently I saw a policeman being importuned by a short, fat lady who tried to make him dance with her. She was overjoyed and capered about enthusiastically, but he kept his usual immovable expression and refused to dance. Suddenly the whole crowd surrounding them gave a loud cheer and joined the lady, forming a circle with the policeman in the centre. They danced and sang happily, but I watched the centre with even more interest and admiration. I could not describe his expression, but somehow he did not strike me as a person in a terribly embarassing situation. Afterwards I tried to make a cartoon recording this impression. (Plate XIVa.)

The London taxi is known for its antiquity by comparison with those in Paris and New York. It is not only its form which keeps up this reputation but the drivers too.

They are generally old and rather crabbed and stubborn, in some way typical of the "English bulldog" in his obstinacy and slowness. I once wanted to catch a certain train and the old driver told me there would be plenty of time for it. On our way to the station, I said to him that we would save time if he drove along a certain road which I happened to know well, but he doggedly kept to his own way. When we reached the station the train had left four minutes ago. The driver remarked that it couldn't be helped. I made no comment but enjoyed the chance of making one more study of a London face.

The salesmen at the Caledonian Market and the newspapermen in the busiest streets are always attracting my attention, not only because their faces and gestures are colourful and paintable, but because their special language, known as "cockney," is so full of charm and picturesqueness! Generally I do not understand what they mean, but they provide me with a great deal for study. Whenever I discovered a word of what they were saying, it was always a joy to me. I do not want to take up space here discussing what I know of Londoners' cockney, but I think London's life would be much duller if it lacked this expressive kind of language. For instance, the jokes in *Punch* would seldom draw a laugh from its readers without the help of cockney. Cockney has an admirable tendency to reduce polysyllables to monosyllables, and to light on expressions that immediately hit the point. For example, to replace "quite" or "rather" by "not 'arf" is an extraordinary improvement in vividness of meaning. I have been to the Caledonian Market several times. I went there before the gate was opened one Tuesday morning. All the salesmen were gathered round the gate with their wheelbarrows and belongings, and they joked with each other in their special language in the highest spirits. I never get tired of listening to it, because it is somewhat musical and not so monotonous as the regularly spoken "King's English." As soon as the gate was opened, of course, they all poured in, without disorder, though each was anxious to occupy a good position if possible. While they were settling down and arranging their things, they were for the moment the happiest creatures in the world. They were hopeful about the coming day and had no thought of any bitter and difficult time in the future. Oh, how I wish all could be like that all their lives! This reminds me, too, of my happy experiences at Covent Garden Market. I had to get up and be there before six o'clock in the morning, otherwise there would not be much to see. I think the greengrocers are even happier than the market salesmen, because they are only there to buy their stuff. I expect most Londoners are still deep in dreams at that hour.

The London newspapermen are always able to sell their papers if they have good positions, because Londoners seem to read an immense amount of them. The newspapermen seem sometimes to be bawling their heads off about a certain piece of news on their placard, but actually they never lose their carefree manner whether the people buy or not. Once or twice about four o'clock in the afternoon I have seen a man hurrying down from Charing Cross Road to Oxford Street corner, breathing hard and with perspiration streaming down his face. He said not a word to the newspaperman, but laid down all the papers and stamped "stop-press news" with a square wooden block on one paper after the other. After he had finished with one newspaper man, he would quickly run to the next one and do the same and then to the third, and so on. His work was very accurate and efficient and I followed him nearly to Oxford Circus station. He had never spoken one word nor made a single pause. I really wanted to stop him for a minute and ask whether he enjoyed his work. Oh, what a life!

There is another type of man in London who is always near my heart. He is the old coalman. Sitting behind his carthorse, bending his back to drive the animal, his face grimy and matching the colour of his oily black coat so that his eyes shine brighter than usual, he shouts out: "Co-al! Co-al!" His slow melodious cry echoes in harmony with the horse's steps up or down the road in the early morning. I used to live in Upper Park Road and now I live in Parkhill Road near Hampstead Heath, where there is only an occasional car passing, so I can enjoy looking at the coalman most times of the year. I sometimes run downstairs and out of the door to walk along the road and meet the cart coming from the other end if it is raining. In rain the scene becomes pathetic and the happy atmosphere is wrapped in sorrow. The old coalman never has an umbrella and the horse seems to amble much more slowly. I could not help making a sketch of the view in rain. (Plate IVb.) I have never spoken to the old man and he seems not to know there is any other type of life besides his own. He shows no different expression from morning to morning and year to year. I am inclined to think that his type has not changed much since his fore-fathers of Charles Dickens's time. Probably the well-paved road does not make more impression on him than the unmade ones. When I meet the scene, I am always re-minded of the description of London in Charles Dickens's novels. And I also wonder if this old man feels cold himself while he sells the coal for others' fires. Do the people who sit by the fireside know about him?

When I travelled to work by tube at the time most London business men do in the early morning, I used not to look at papers very much, because I was busy watching people coming in or getting out at various stations. Nearly everyone had a paper in his hand, but the amusing thing for me was to watch those who wore glasses. Someone would get in, sit down, take out a handkerchief to dust his clothes, and then take off his glasses, wipe them and put them in a case. Afterwards he would take out another case, put on another pair of glasses and begin to unfold the newspaper. But this takes time and realising that the next station would be his, he would take off the second pair of glasses again, put on the first pair and prepare to get out. I saw this on many an occasion, and took a great fancy to the different types of English spectacles. There are two types I always like very much, one is the pince-nez and the other the monocle. I cannot help looking with fascination at people who just put them on and off with a mere twitch of the nose! I wanted very much to possess either of those kinds, so I went to an optician and made special inquiries. But the answer was that my eyes and nose were unsuitable for either the one or the other. It was a great disappointment to me, but I was glad I was made to realise that I was staying in a foreign country, where there were things which did not fit my eyes and nose. I wonder if the people who go to China realise that there is always something which cannot fit everyone's eyes and nose in that country too!

"To a foreigner," says Mr. Burgin, "it is a positive pleasure to see an Englishman sitting, or rather lying, in one of those couch-like contrivances by the fireside in an English club." Yes, this is absolutely true, but I wonder how he knows it if he himself is English. I have been taken to many different clubs such as the Athenaeum, Grosvenor, Arts, Fine Art, and so on, but I generally refrained from talking to my friends and tried to steal some glances at the people in the corners of the room or by the fireside. Mostly they are old men with bald heads and white beards sitting back comfortably and closing their eyes, as if to say: "Thank God, I can have a little peace here." I suppose bright young men are seldom attracted to such places. I have tried to make a study of English clubs, and though I have found no ancient records, I would like to suggest that English clubs were started by hen-pecked husbands. People may argue with me, but they

A Chinese henpecked husband

cannot tell me why clubs have not allowed ladies to enter until very recently, and some of the old clubs still keep this rule. Whenever I see a couple walking in the street or a photograph reproduced in papers, I generally have the feeling that the lady looks triumphant and domineering while the gentleman is very timid and diffident standing by her side. By no means do I see any harm in being a henpecked husband and I really think it is a good charac-teristic in a man to be able to become so. We Chinese are naturally so if married, and are preparing to be if still un-married. I think that is a reason why the Chinese race has been maintained without any break through five thousand years! No invader can conquer us because we have many good hens, and I am very proud to say it. There are endless stories written in books on the subject and I have heard thousands of them. It is said there was a well-known scholar who once invited a few of his good friends to come round to his garden for a happy afternoon. They met in a pavilion which was quite apart from the main building, so they knew their talk could not be heard by the lady of the family. Those friends all knew this gentleman as a fine example of that henpecked type of husband, so they began to joke about it and to tease him for being so. But this gentleman tried very hard to defend himself, and shouted out in a very triumphant manner that he had treated his wife in this and that way. While he was making these statements he suddenly fell off his seat in terror, because he had heard a sharp call from his wife ordering him in, and all the friends slipped away secretly by the back door. There is another story which runs as follows:

"Ten henpecked husbands formed themselves into a sworn society for resisting the poisonous oppression of their wives. At the first meeting, they were sitting talking over their pipes and wine, when suddenly the ten wives, who had got wind of the movement, appeared on the scene. There was a general stampede, and nine of the husbands incontinently bolted like rats through a side door, only one remaining unmoved to face the music. The ladies merely smiled contemptuously at the success of their raid, and went away. The nine husbands then agreed that the bold tenth man, who had not run away, should be appointed their president; but on coming to offer him the post, they found that he had died of fright."[1]

I suppose the English menfolk have no pavilion in which to talk in private, so they have to have their club. I do not know whether they talk as we do, but I imagine that they must have some fun too. Inevitable changes have turned the clubs into a special kind of restaurant, so this fun perhaps does not exist any more.

In most clubs, there is always an atmosphere of smoke if

[1] Translated by Prof. Giles.

not of spirit. Several times I have felt tempted to try an English pipe, but I have never actually done so. I like to look at it when it hangs out of the corner of a person's mouth. Though there are no more servants like those who poured a bucket of water over Sir Walter Raleigh, yet I am sure that there is someone like Sir James Barrie who wrote *My Lady Nicotine*. A French author has said that "The cigarette is the perfect type of pleasure, because it leaves one just unsatisfied." I believe nine out of ten Londoners would agree.

There is one thing about the English club which I still cannot understand. A friend of mine came to my house one day and we had a good talk about all kinds of subjects. Suddenly he told me that he was delighted beyond words that on that very day he had become a member of the cricket club. He went on to tell me that his father had put his name down as a candidate for membership of that club, when he was just born, but he had never had the chance to join before. He is now nearly forty years of age and it is at last his turn to become a member. I can still remember the joy on his face when he was telling me this. But I really do not see why he is so fearfully anxious to be that member, although I know he likes sport very much. This kind of thing is beyond my knowledge.

Londoners love to wear uniforms, though they claim to have a ban on them. But the kind I mean are not the uniforms of a political party. London butchers wear a uniform, chefs too, page boys too, waiters and waitresses too, and many others. Those who pin their rows of decorations on the uniforms, and stand in front of a hotel or a big restaurant, are an admirable sight with their lordly bearing, and are certainly typical of London. They always give me clear directions if I ask my way. But the worst type of uniform I myself have to wear sometimes is the evening dress—"tails" and "dinner-jacket," and all that. I have never tried to see what a top-hat would look like on my head, but I have had enough unbearable experiences with wearing a high, hard collar and starched shirt. Those things almost bring tears to my eyes, because my head becomes immovable and my body feels as if bandaged; and besides, when I eat or drink I have the greatest discomfort in swallowing. Once I went to a dinner at the Forum Club, and I was upset to find that my only starched shirt had been sent to the laundry a few days before. As soon as I got to the dinner, I prepared to tell the story of this when it was my turn to speak. By bad luck, the gentleman in front of me spoke about that very same misfortune, so I had to think of a different topic. Once I was given a ticket to a lecture at the Royal Institute, but I did not know the audience ought to wear uniform, either jacket or tails; so I felt embarrassed at being the only one there without either. Ah, uniform of jacket and tails! I may be mistaken, but it seems to me that any kind of official meeting or official dinner imposes this uniform on its members to differentiate them from common people—a kind of social snobbery. Why should everyone be dressed so? I suppose this is also a way of training menfolk to become henpecked.

Every Londoner appears to go out to business in the morning and get back for a meal in the evening, or he may have a drink at a public bar or spend an hour or two at the cinema or somewhere else, and at the week-end he may drive into the country or stay a night there, and so his life goes on in the same routine. I think he should always be happy and without any worry at all. But "life" is a very curious thing. It is made of interruptions and worries, and the mystery of it has never been solved by any philosopher either in the West or in the East. So I feel that

Londoners probably have all kinds of worries as we Chinese have, in living, sickness, birth, and death, and the rest; but it seems to me that they have one extra worry of which we have not dreamed, and which I do not think will ever come to us. That is the *worry of happiness*. I have found, for instance, that most rich Londoners worry about hotels where they are to spend their holidays; the middle-class man who may just have enough money to make himself happy, worries over not being able to afford the expensive way to happiness or because he thinks he is not properly treated or well respected at big parties; and the poor ones worry over not having enough amusement and entertainment. They all clamour for "fun," and they keep striving for it and remain constantly unsatisfied. I have enough worries on my own account, as I now begin to realise the implications of "life" more and more, but I do not think I have ever had the *worry of happiness* here. During these past two years, my worries have grown, and besides my personal failures I have to worry about the ruthless war which is being waged on our land and people, the death of my brother, the moving about and the scattering of the members of my big family, the damage done to our properties, the flood in my native city, and so on. Naturally I have not had much time for worrying about happiness. One might think that it is a horrible idea to disclaim happiness, but how could I do otherwise? Yet I can have joy from time to time, because I can work. While I work, I keep myself aloof from most worries. Perhaps my work is the only form of happiness I have now. If I cannot get away for a rest, I can go up to Hampstead Heath for a little while. If I cannot have a look at the trees on the Heath, I can enjoy watching the movement of the leaves on a tree in front of my window. This is my life in London! Alas, there is so big a difference in life between man and man!

In the course of my five years' stay in London I really have acquired much admiration for the English character. One day I met Dr. C. C. Wang, the chairman of the Chinese Association in London, who has been here much longer than I have and has also been to other places in Europe and America. We had a good talk together; then I asked him what he thought about English people. He said that they had many good points, which could be summed up in the three words *"pardon," "thanks,"* and *"please."* I endorse his opinion. Those three words are on their lips every minute as they go about their work and bring up their youngsters. He then added that English people *never get excited.* Indeed, they have passed through many crises in these last five years, but they just carry on as usual. What impresses me most is their efficiency and persistence in carrying out their work. I have many personal experiences in dealing with English business people and find they carry out their task in a most efficient way, though it may be a little slow. I have observed efficiency and calmness and persistence in the English, and I know many English people who have shown me by example how to remain firm against all kinds of bitterness. I am grateful to them, but I think the "endurance of bitterness" is the chief characteristic of the Chinese race and one which has never been broken for the last five thousand years. Our history tells of many kinds of difficulties and bitterness endured but we have always won through. Our forefathers have never told their descendants to enjoy life first, but rather to taste the bitterness of it before they can enjoy. My family goes back as far as the end of the first century before Christ, and we keep a long record in our clan book. In that book there is a rule for the whole family, consisting of only four words written by our first ancestor. Those four words are "benevolence," "righteousness," "sincerity," and "endurance." Each member of the family should be trained to carry out these four qualities. I used to be scolded by my grandparents and parents if I chose the best thing for myself first and left the less good for others. They said we should taste the bitterness first. Probably no Englishman would agree with this, but I must say we shall have to taste more bitterness than usual from now on. I have always been ready to do so and shall teach our next generation this lesson as well. An ancient Chinese parable which has always been taught to us generation after generation may illustrate the Chinese character well:

A certain Mr. Blockhead whose home faced the great mountains T'ai Hsing and Wang-Wo. In his old age he made a plan to level out the mountains entirely so that he might have communication with the outside world. His family agreed to help him, so he started forthwith to dig up the mountains and wheel the earth away into the sea. But one of his neighbours began to deride him saying, "In your extreme old age you won't even be able to lift a feather from the ground, how can you hope to tackle all the rocks and earth?" Mr. Blockhead retorted, "If I die my son will survive me, and my son will bring grandsons into the world, and they in their turn will multiply, while these mountains have stopped growing many hundreds of years ago." The wiseacre could find no answer to the argument. The story goes on to say that the God of Mountains reported Mr. Blockhead's remarks to the Supreme Being, who arranged for the mountains to be cleared away by supernatural intervention.

We tell this story to illustrate the persistence of the Chinese character, and so long as there are any Mr. Block-heads left in our land we shall never cease uprooting unwanted invaders!

未睡日觀雪
誰知汝獨先
斯時應輸汝
聊以待來年

Translation of the poem is on page 81

On Women

I am a man. How can I say anything about woman? Lord Byron says: "What a strange thing is man! And what a stranger is woman!" From my own experience he is right. Though I know many women friends as well as the female members of my family, yet I am constantly making new discoveries about them and probably will never understand them fully. The whole activity of the human world is virtually controlled not by man but woman, whether in the West or East. When I was a child at home, I thought my grandmother was the most powerful person in the world. Every member of the family had to obey her and even if the aged grandfather wanted to take me out with him to air his birds, he had to get her consent. She was always smiling and never lost her temper with anyone. She did not force anyone to obey her, but we all obeyed her absolutely. I cannot take up space here to describe how she achieved this, but I can say that she controlled us in perfect manner. Were she alive, I should not be able to stay here in London unless she agreed. We boys were only allowed to occupy ourselves in studying the classics and were not instructed in the secret of dealing with matters inside the house, but my sister and cousins received special instruction from her on how to become a good house-ruler. Sometimes my sister or cousin, even one of my aunts, would raise a protest against some dictum of hers, to which she would reply: "You are right. When I was your age I thought as you do now, but you will feel differently when you reach my age. And you must remember that you will all become the rulers of houses one day, then you will see the difficulties." After that, nobody would say anything more and they just accepted her decree.

Since my arrival here I have realised more and more the power of women. I have become used to the etiquette of "ladies first." Everywhere I go and at any gathering I join there are generally more women than men. Once I tried to do a very stupid thing, to count the shops which sold women's goods from Oxford Circus down to Regent's Street at the end of Piccadilly Circus and then on to Green Park, but I had to give it up one-third of the way. The result would be the same if I tried to count them along Oxford Street or New Bond Street or any street in London. Most spaces in the papers are filled with things concerning women. The women themselves have a word to say. Miss Cicely Hamilton, the authoress, once claimed before an audience of women that women were the stronger sex. "We have to pay," she said, "the highest rates of insurance because we survive the longest and are the most difficult to kill." The other day I saw a book called *Men are so hopeless*! I seem to remember that one or two years ago there was an American lady clamouring about changing the power from men's hands to women's. There must be many others of the same mind in facing the present restless, ruthless world and perhaps they have been fighting for that goal for a long time. I quite agree with them, and there must be scores of men who would like to become subjects, as they have never ceased praising and paying compliments to ladies' cleverness. But why have women never got into real power so far? I cannot understand it. The men, including myself, who praise them must be using empty words. I myself cannot answer.

I have grown interested in reading about fashions, hats, dress, make-up, and so forth. The more I read, the more

I am puzzled. Though a woman may admit that she is not as beautiful as some others, yet she is quite convinced that she will be able to attract a man. But if this is so, why is she always thinking about beautifying herself? If she is convinced of her own beauty why should she still be thinking about increasing it? I doubt whether women can get the real power into their hands if they spend so much more time on beautifying themselves than men. One paper says that in 1935, ninety-five out of every hundred women used face powder, as against twenty out of every hundred fifteen years earlier. And in the same time, the proportion of those having a permanent wave had risen from one in 200 to sixty in 100; thirty-five out of every hundred used rouge and lipstick as against six in 1921.

The other day, the paper said that bad weather during the last few years has taught some women to take precautions, and it was not unusual to see smart racegoers arriving complete with hatbox. If the weather kept fine the comparatively simple hat worn on arrival can always be exchanged for a more elaborate "creation" about the time the King and Queen are due to arrive. I wonder whether the King and Queen have time to look at the elaborate hats? I also wonder whether the ladies like the people to look at their hats or their faces. It is always interesting to me that I have very seldom seen any two hats alike during these five years. I took a great fancy to some of them. The Chinese coolie hat some ladies have adopted sends my thoughts home and I seem to see our men with changed sex! Ever since the success of the play *Lady Precious Stream*, a man's hat became a woman's fashion. And since the exhibition of Chinese Art, some Chinese words, or supposed Chinese, have been embroidered on women's garments. Once I was taken to a very expensive little hat-shop somewhere in the West End, because a lady

I knew wanted me to choose the right colour for her. It was a very difficult job for which I was not equal, but I enjoyed listening to the conversation between the ladies. There were four smart young girls serving the customers, two for an old lady with pure white hair and two for the one whom I accompanied. They talked without ceasing, and every word spoken by the four girls was to inspire and encourage the visitors to buy the hats. They were very clever in finding words to describe the colour, shape, fashion, and fitting of the hats for each visitor, and were quick to follow the visitors' idea. I learned many expressions of which I would never have thought myself, but I could not repeat them. I was asked to give my opinion from time to time but I could say nothing except "nice," "excellent," etc., because I know nothing about ladies' hats at all. I wished I could have remembered some of the good expressions among those which I heard the perfect English gentleman address to young ladies at parties. However, I managed to say a few words without blushing too much. Finally the old lady bought two stylish hats and went away. Then my friend ordered two to be specially made for her. We had spent nearly two hours in the shop. I remarked to my friend that she had a very beautiful hat on her head at the moment so why did she want to have two more newly made, and I had heard English people were proud of being unostentatious. She replied that ladies had to have plenty of different hats, or life would be too dull. Oh, what about men's hats?

Once I read a title of an article in a paper: "Girls want more courage for charming clothes." This surprised me for I have always thought the contrary. I feel girls and women are the more daring sex, and would wear anything if they thought it added to their charm and beauty. For instance, I saw a photograph of a spectator at motor-races wearing a hat with a small racing car on it. I felt it would surely fall off and her head seemed overloaded with it, but she did not care.

"Clothes tell the story," writes Mrs. Alison Settle, "of what is in our minds, our lives, with changes almost as quick as the movies. They always have done so, but only those able to purchase expensive books and pictures used to be made aware of that fact in old days. Now every girl and woman in the country knows that this year skirts tend to be shorter, shoulders square or wide, to balance the return of the pinched waist and the wider or the pleated skirt."

If women had no courage who would lead the change? Every English woman wants to wear something different from the others, because she is thoroughly confident of herself. I was once struck by a lady who wore an old Chinese embroidered robe at a party. She was very proud of her gown as she moved round from group to group, especially when she was admired by her fellow guests; but I am inclined to wonder what English people would think of a small and short Chinese lady wearing an Elizabethan type of costume picked up from the drawer of a repertory theatre. I can almost imagine that the head of the lady would not even emerge from the huge skirt. Probably a Chinese lady would not have

The head of the Chinese lady would not even emerge from the Elizabethan skirt

the courage to wear it among her friends. Though I like to look at ladies' evening dresses, yet there is one little objection to them—I do not know how to move my feet while I follow them back to the seats after an interval in a theatre or go in to dinner at a big dinner-party. If I step forward a little too much, I shall be tramping on the long trailing skirt of the lady in front of me and she will stop with a jerk, not even looking round, while the people behind me will start back too. If I move a little more slowly I shall be pushed along by those behind. I escape this miserable experience in my own country!

Though Mr. C. R. W. Nevinson said that in history the inspiration of artists had been, not women, but first food, then fear, then religion, and that sex only entered in after thousands of years, I am inclined to think that women have taken part in literature earlier than in art. It is strange that in most cases the women described and painted are a few chosen ones who have been considered pleasing and beautiful to the majority of men. The poets and artists begin to describe their ideal women. Then women imitate as far as they are able. If they have not natural faces and figures to reach that standard, they try to make-up by what is usually described as "the tricks for beauty." But, alas, no poets or artists have ever noticed or cared that they have neglected a large number of women, leaving them to despair and to end their lives tragically. I have read many cases in the daily papers here about girls dying through slimming. Let us just think of the bitterness of those who cannot "slim" and those who cannot be beautiful by make-up at all. It is considered cruel to keep a dog and not give him enough food when he is hungry. Oh, my fellow poets and artists, how could you make so many girls give up eating to achieve slimness? To my surprise, I saw an organisation called "National Slimming

Campaign" advertised at Great Newport Street. This is why I said that women are the more daring sex, because they even do not mind dying for slimness. Of course, many doctors and chemists have made large fortunes from it!

The modern tendency in art has given a turn to the conception of womanly beauty, for the moderns paint and sculpt them naturally. I think this ought to be liked by the majority of women, if not by men. But I am told there are still some who regret not having been born in Africa, the West Indies, and so on, so that they may have a tan-coloured skin. I can hardly understand all these intricacies!

I think I am myself a good supporter of the "Women's Movement" in China. More than ten years ago, I used to edit a weekly women's supplement for a newspaper at Hangchow, the beautiful West-Lake city in China. Once I wrote an article called "Why does man always keep his eyes on girls?" In that article I quoted many expressions describing women's eyes, mouths, hair, arms, fingers, waist, feet, clothes, etc., from the earliest literature we have until the present day; and said that the writers would not be able to describe them so closely if they did not look at the girls with particular attention. Why should that happen and the girls allow it to be so? It seemed to me that girls were always in the hands of men to be made fun of and played with. After that article was published there was a great storm, and I was directly attacked by a number of writers, poets, and Chinese artists of the new school. The common point was that women are not immortals and angels, and even if they were, men would have the right to talk about them, especially as women like to be talked about. Strangely enough, there was a lady writer who wrote me a very sarcastic letter about how women talked of men, in which she described men in a most witty style, but unfortunately she did not appear able to give sufficient concrete illustrations. I received those hits and published them all, but I was not satisfied because they did not deal with me on the point at issue. Later I met an old professor of mine who had taught me for a long time, and one of whose poems describing the limpid, sparkling eyes of ladies had been quoted in my article. Smoothing his white beard and smiling, he said to me that my article was excellent, but I would know why men like to talk about women and they liked to be talked about, when I grew older. Oh, this growing older! I do not mean that women and men should not talk about and describe each other—that is part of the human treasure of freedom—but I mean to say that we men had better not encourage the ladies to alter and confine their natural qualities to pander to our taste so that large numbers are in agony. I prefer natural beauties and I am still of the same way of thinking, though I am older now. But since I have been here, I begin to notice that any lady I know in London would gladly receive a compliment on her beauty. If I wrote an article such as I just mentioned I should be hissed away!

I like to talk with London womenfolk, whenever I meet them and when they want to talk to me. They ask me many interesting questions which I could never think of myself and which I may not be able to answer, but they have taught me also to realise that there are many different minds in the world. Once I met a lady journalist and we talked a good while at a party. I gathered she was an expert on beauty when she began to ask me what I thought of *make-up*. I said I had no objection to it, but I wished people would not try too hard if their faces were not suited to make-up. Then I told her a story about "crude imitation:"

"Hsi Shih (the most renowned beauty in Chinese history), knit her brows at the whole district during an attack of heart disease. An ugly hag in the neighbourhood happened to see her in that attitude, and Hsi Shih's charm so struck her that on returning to her village she forthwith strove also to knit her brows with one hand pointing to the heart. At the sight of this would-be beauty, the rich of that place shut their doors so fast so as not to venture out again, while the poor had to flee from her with their families."[1]

There was another lady with whom I used to talk a great deal. From time to time she seemed to notice that I had not much interest in jewels, so when her husband had given her a new diamond ring or some other trinket, she would just show it to her other friends and tell them with a finger pointing at me: "This young man never wants to look at jewels." I admitted that I knew nothing about them, but I gave no explanation. We saw plays together on several occasions. In the intervals she always asked me to look at this and that lady's dress while we were standing in the hall, and wanted to have my opinion. I generally answered "nice," but she was not satisfied with that. When she insisted, I said: "We are here to look at the play, aren't we?" Again, she noticed that I very seldom looked at others while we were walking in the parks and streets, and she then said: "Surely you must have liked to look at girls in China? Are English girls much different from Chinese? Don't you like to look at them? It is usually man's instinct and habit." I was surprised at her remark, but I answered her promptly: "Yes, I like to look at them as well as I did in my own country. But I like to look at them *from behind*, because I prefer to leave the other side to

[1] Translated by Dr. K. T. Sen.

my imagination." At that she burst into laughter. It is true that I always like to look at women when they are walking in front of me, especially when there are only a few people on the road. I can enjoy looking at their graceful gait, added to their admirable English figure which rarely gives any indication of age. And the sound of their footsteps on the pavement is also charming to listen to.

To follow a lady shopping in a big store is quite interesting, but one experience is enough. About two years ago I was asked by a young lady to go with her to Liberty's for some Chinese porcelains. Before we reached the right department she stopped at the stockings, handerkerchiefs, umbrella, and perfume counters on the way. Most of the things were quite unfamiliar to me, so I was always at a loss to answer questions. She seemed to think that I would know more about the porcelains, so at last we got there. I tried to answer as many of her questions as I could, but soon I was tired of saying anything, because my mouth was very dry inside. Then she said: "This I like, because its colour is nice. And that I also like, because it has a beautiful design on it. But the one on that table is decorative and good for a small room. . . ." When she made her decision and bought one small jar, we had been in the shop about an hour and a half!

A young Chinese lady told me one day that old ladies in England are very fond of gossiping. They could talk together for about two or three hours even if they had never known each other before. And some of them would criticise the young girls who smoke and use powder and lip-stick. She further said that most English spinsters have queer ways, but that they were all very kind. Their fussing over small things was unbearable. About all these things I know nothing. But I think most young English girls are very good at gossiping too. At parties, at exhibitions, at shows, and so forth, I very seldom hear a man's voice. Once I went to call on a friend at a hotel in Half Moon Street, and was put to wait in a drawing-room. There were four young girls talking there. My friend was apparently detained for some reason, and did not come down for about half an hour. Within that time I do not think those girls ceased talking one minute. I always wonder why they have so much to say, and I wonder also why men are less talkative. On the whole English girls are active, able, and sincere, but rather severe also! And for some reason I generally feel they have faces which reveal a dominating character. Baron Kurt von Stutterheim says: "The Englishman has a rooted objection to marrying for money, so that girls who are rolling in wealth often remain unmarried. The Englishwoman is more calculating." I wonder whether my explanation of a "domineering" face may be the reason why those Englishmen have avoided marrying wealthy girls?

Jealousy is an inborn defect of human beings. I do not think women are the only culprits, but they perhaps have more than men or have it in a different form. There is a jealousy in the human race as well as in nations, in ideologies, in professions, in political parties, and in personal lives. I think the last kind is the most common among ladies. To my mind, jealousy may be a virtue if there is not too much of it present, and it is often interesting to see a lady in a jealous mood. I think there is some difference in the degree of this quality in English and Chinese girls; certainly they have different methods of showing it. A Chinese girl may prevent her lover or husband from yielding to temptation by softening his heart by silence or by kind advice, but the English girl, I gather from the newspapers, will fight openly by reprisals or by breaking off her relationship. I may be wrong in both cases, but anyway these situations are just what make life at once more colourful and more difficult to endure. In China, we interpret "jealousy" by means of the expression "eating vinegar." It is said a well-known prime minister of T'ang dynasty had never had any chance to let his eyes stray to pretty girls, because his wife was furiously jealous. But the emperor recognised the great services he had done for the empire, and thought he should have a joyful time in his old age. So he sent the abstemious minister two court girls, because he had no son to carry on his family. The minister hesitated to receive them, and the emperor, on learning about his jealous wife, summoned her to the court. Preparing a cup of poison on the royal table, the emperor asked the wife whether she preferred to drink the cup or to curb her jealousy. She made no answer, but just went up to the table and drained the cup at one draught. Then the emperor shook his head, sighed, and said: "Even a man who has as great power as I have cannot deal with a woman's jealousy!" Afterwards the liquid in the cup was found to be not poison but vinegar, so since then vinegar has come to mean "jealousy." Another explanation for the term is that we generally call a jealous woman a roaring lion, because of her manner and voice, and we traditionally believe that a lion likes to drink a large quantity of vinegar. I cannot describe how an English woman behaves when she is jealous, so I must try to get some experienced menfolk to tell me. But I believe in England there is always jealousy among the ladies themselves. The gossip of old ladies about the younger ones and the younger's retort to the old certainly show signs of it.

Before I came over here, I was given the impression that women stood higher than men and were more highly respected by them in the West than in the East. Since I

have been here and have tried to observe things for myself,
I think my hearsay impression must be corrected. It is
quite true that women have every advantage in social life,
such as at parties, in conferences, in travelling, and so forth,
because of the tradition "Ladies first." Again they have
equal opportunity with men in getting employment. And
they have the same training as men, so that they can stand
independently—a system for which I have nothing to say
but admiration. But here comes my question. Is women's
life exactly equal with that of men on the physical as well
as on the mental side? I am not putting this question for
girls who have rich parents or relatives or have inherited
a large sum of money, but I am trying to think of those who
live from hand to mouth. In London I often hear that
women get less pay than men and the employers always
have a tendency to employ girls, because they are cheaper.
Why is it so? I begin to think that women and men do not
stand on the same level. I also hear that the self-opinion-
ated manager or the small director—the man they call
"boss"—sometimes treats and scolds the girls very badly.
High positions seldom have a good effect upon character,
especially in the business world. I have had many experiences of this treatment myself, and I had to endure it
because I had to live. But I think for girls it is very
difficult to bear without distress. Once I read a case about
a big firm, where a girl worker had been falsely accused of
stealing by an inspector. They fined her according to the
regulation, but actually it turned out to be a mistake.
From that time the girl's reputation went down in the firm
and she could not get on with her work because everybody
joked about her. Although the firm was then fined in
return to restore the girl's name, yet I cannot help thinking
there must be some other cases like this, but where the
girls did not bring abuses to light for fear of losing their

jobs. Again I am thinking that there is a great difference in the physical elements of women and men. Everyone has the physical need that nature has planted in them, though those who have to work hard for a living may not have time to satisfy it. This predicament becomes more difficult for women than for men, as men's age does not matter, while women will not easily get married after a certain time. Women have to spend the prime of their life fighting for a living and it will not come again, even though they may have saved a little money for their own enjoyment. So they drift into a life of singleness, loneliness, and restless dissatisfaction. I think this is against nature, but it is not the women's fault at all.

To my surprise, Dr. Leonard Williams says about women teachers: "The women who have the responsibility of teaching these girls are, many of them, themselves embittered, sexless or homosexual hoydens who try to mould the girls into their own pattern." I am not in a position to discuss the matter with Dr. Williams, but I think he is not being just. As a foreigner from China, I feel that English women have not been esteemed highly by men in the fundamental sense. I think that no Chinese would dare to accuse our educated womenfolk in such a public and rude way. To me it seems as if there is constant joking about spinsters in London, but why do people not try to put themselves into the spinsters' position and to experience their life? The granting of pensions to spinsters is a difficult problem for Parliament. But why? They may be very happy, and have no queer habits, but they are certainly not born to like a single life. Some of them may have had unfortunate love affairs, and prefer to live a lonely life, but most of them, I gather, were overwhelmed with work and had no chance. To fall in love and get married is no easy job. I hear there used to be spinsters going round St. Pancras seeking for husbands, but what a life! And how could people joke about it? English women have the same worries as men have, including that of happiness, but they have some more. They have to worry about hats, shoes, clothes, make-up, and about loneliness if they are spinsters. They have more sense of vanity and they have to look after their self-respect. Sometimes it makes me feel thoroughly wretched when I think of those women leading their monotonous lives. A man who finishes his office work can go about to find entertainment as he likes anywhere and at any time, but for women it is different. Though they are as free as men, yet they are confined by many conventional ideas. If they do not earn enough to afford to go to a theatre or cinema, they have to stay in their little pigeon-nest room hour after hour. Going on like this all through life until death comes, what real enjoyment can one have? Oh, life, it is difficult for every-body. But I am inclined to think it has been always even more difficult for women than men. Our Chinese women may have suffered a great deal from lack of freedom in the old days, but they all hoped to become the rulers of houses and to be served and highly respected by their sons and daughters. Now they enjoy equal rights and as much freedom as English women enjoy, and they can still expect to become rulers of houses as well, and to have filial children.

I do not want to think that we must come to an entirely mechanised form of life one day, yet I would like to see the system of every individual working independently adopted in my country. But certainly we should find a great remedy for women's lot! Oh, English women, I hope you will not misunderstand what I mean about you being un-happy. Many of you are happy enough, but I hope those who have too much happiness will think of the unhappy ones. Especially men, do not joke about women!

康林紅似犬下有綠陰鋪
松風吹謖謖涼意立襟裾
少女自幽絕獨坐看情書
白鵝不解事時窺林隅

康林漫步 呦
康林

Translation of the poem is on page 30

On Old Age

It is strange that we Chinese do not mind at all when we are complimented on "becoming older," but Londoners will be furious about it. This reminds me of a Chinese parable which runs as follows:

"Once upon a time there lived a rich man in the State of Sung, the walls of whose house had partly collapsed as the result of a heavy rainfall. 'If the damage is not repaired,' admonished his son, 'I am sure there will be robbers.' This argument was supported by their neighbour's father. That very night the man was actually deprived of the major portion of his wealth exactly as his son had feared. After the event, he thought highly of his son's foresight, but suspected his neighbour!"[1]

It is difficult to pass any comment! But why are people so unwilling to see other's point of view?

I myself have always looked forward to becoming older, especially when I was in the Chinese Civil Service. As we are brought up in the Confucian idea of "filial piety" as well as "respect for elders," elders enjoy every kind of privilege in Chinese society. Wherever they go and whatever they want to undertake, they always stand a better chance, because they are considered to have more experience. A well-known Chinese saying declares that no word is reliable if one has no hairs on one's mouth. I have

---

[1] Translated by Dr. K. T. Sen.

suffered from this deficiency! When I was appointed to be in charge of the local government at Wuhu, I was about twenty-five years of age. When I first arrived to take up office, I was greeted by a large group of elderly men, mostly with white beards and white hair, who were the heads of villages and of towns. Unfortunately they did not convey the usual message of greeting and express the people's hope that the new governor would do good throughout the district; they just kept silent and went away after a while. I felt no curiosity about their conduct, but afterwards I was told that they thought I was too young for the post. After three years I was moved from that district and took up office in my birthplace, Kiukiang. Experience had made me cautious and I tried to grow a beard, because everybody kept saying that they remembered me as a child not so long ago. It was a great nuisance to me that my beard grew very slowly and sparsely so that I hardly looked any older after a few months. And it became a subject for joking. After I gave up office I shaved my beard off at once! Talking about beards, I read a very interesting passage in the *Evening Standard* one day:

"Capt. L. C. Schlotel, an anti-gas expert, speaking at Plymouth about air raid precautions, said: 'It is difficult to fit bearded men with gas masks, and should an emergency arise, those with beards more than a hand long might be faced with the alternative of either cutting their beards off or being gassed.' Bearded men have varying views about this statement. Mr. George Bernard Shaw said: 'I prefer to chance it. I am certainly not going to cut my beard off and I am rather sceptical about gas masks. I dislike the style of their appearance. I have never, never shaved and I am not going to start now. I have saved a lot of time.' And Mr. Frank

Brangwyn said: 'This has come rather suddenly. I want time to consider whether or not I would cut off my beard in case of emergency'."

This is something to mark the modern age. I quite agree with Mr. Shaw that the appearance of the gas mask is not agreeable, but I wonder whether he has thought that after his time there may be a fashion for a gas-mask type of face? I can imagine in a few years' time that there will be no bearded men, and people may even find gas masks or their equivalent a fashionable item of apparel. But I have gone far away from my subject, and a beard is not the only sign of old age!

Though Londoners do not like to be called old, yet there are some offices for which older men are preferable. Before Mr. Anthony Eden took office as Secretary for Foreign Affairs, there was talk about his age and whether he could be appointed or not. I very seldom see professors at universities who are not old men with white beards and bald heads. They seem to me to have a pride in being old. How strange! They do not like to be addressed as old men, but they behave in a condescending elderly manner if they are addressing a young man. Once when I walked into the staff common-room of the school where I had been teaching, I saw an elderly professor relaxing his body on a sofa with both legs outstretched. His white beard was obvious, as he leaned his head against the back of the sofa. As I was nearing the fireplace, he rubbed his spectacles and said to me, "What subject are you studying?" Apparently he thought I must have come into the wrong room. But I answered: "I should like to study Persian, though I am teaching Chinese here." I often wished to become an old man with a white beard and a bald head like many of the others, while I was teaching there.

I think I actually gave pleasure to some English gentlemen on one occasion. When I was taken to the Arts Guild by Mr. Lowes D. Luard who was to give a lecture there, I saw the ceremony of the new president of the guild taking up office from the retiring one. After that ceremony came the secretary's report on the business which had been done, and he emphasised particularly that the guild would allow young people to become members from that year onwards. After Mr. Luard's lecture, I was called upon to say a few words. Before speaking, I looked round the whole room but could only find three or four people about my age. Then I said:

"After having heard the secretary's report, I did not think any person as young as I am would have the honour to be called upon to speak in this guild. As I come from a country where we respect elders very highly, we young people have to be very careful and do as we are told by our elders. So now I suppose I must make a short speech, but my whole body is trembling before so many elders to-night. . . ."

I do not know whether they were really pleased or not, but I got a cheer. Afterwards I spoke about the important element in Chinese painting which we call "rhythmic vitality," but I did not pronounce the first vowel "i" in vitality correctly. So after my talk, an old member with a long pure white beard stood up to ask whether the word was "vitality" or "fatality." Oh, vitality and fatality are both important to artists nowadays as well as to old gentlemen!

For Englishwomen especially, old age is more fatal than anything. I was warned not to mention anything about age before ladies when I first arrived here. But I have always been amused to hear a gentleman telling an old lady how young she looked. She is certainly pleased, but I think it is more than ironical. "Old age" seems to be poison to girls, and young Chinese girls have the same idea. There is a story about it. It is said that a wealthy man once met a young girl and they became friendly, so he asked her age and she answered that she was eighteen. After he had left her for some years, he met this girl again. But she completely forgot that she had told him her age before, and said that she was seventeen this time when he inquired. To her surprise the man wept bitterly, and the girl could not make out what was the matter. He then explained that he was reminded of how his property was getting less and less every year, just like her age, and that this caused him sadness. I suppose a woman's memory is particularly bad in this respect, because no woman seems to remember when she was born.

About three years ago, there was an amazing account of the life story of a woman of sixty-three who posed as a child-princess of eleven. It is said that she was extremely childish and simple in her behaviour, and in her attitude to the affair altogether, when she was under the doctor's observation on the charge of obtaining money from others under false pretences. Through all these years this woman of sixty-three walked about dressed in short frocks, with her mop of fair hair tied up with a ribbon. The journalist said that the most remarkable fact of all was that so many people believed not only that she was a child but that she was of royal lineage. How could it be so? I know it is quite an unusual case, but I am inclined to think that the people who believed in her must have always wanted to be young themselves, otherwise they could not have been so blind. This dislike of old age gives rise to various methods of keeping young and becoming younger. I occasionally read in the daily papers that clothes can make people look young, and cosmetics and slimming have the same function. And some beauty experts can even tighten up face wrinkles and smooth them away, so that a woman of sixty can look like one of twenty. But why should it be so? I think it is quite contrary to nature. I do not think this form of make-up has ever been known in my country. A woman of forty in China is beginning to be content with her age and does not want to look like a young girl again. It is generally believed that Chinese people, especially women, always look younger than their real age. I think the reason is that we do not worry so much as Westerners do. The more English women worry about keeping young the more easily they really become older, while our Chinese ladies do not work hard and are entirely free of the worry of make-up, but they are content to make themselves beautiful according to their age. I believe they mostly divide their lives into three periods— under thirty, between thirty and fifty, and over fifty. At each period they wear different and suitable colours, ornaments, and jewels, according to traditional ideas. It is said that under thirty they should wear bright light colours and shining materials to indicate youth and vigour, over thirty, darker and less brilliant colours to show that they have settled down and are able to instruct others, and over fifty, plainer dark colours to indicate dignity and command respect. When I was in China I often saw my grandmother and aunts advising my sister and cousins to choose this or that bright-coloured dress, while admitting that they themselves would not like to wear such colours to compete with younger people and lose their dignity. But I remember in *Punch* there was a drawing of a young girl and her mother; and the girl said to her mother: "Mummy, I've come to the conclusion that you are more beautiful than me. What a mercy we're different types!" I do not think that our mothers would ever accept such an idea.

I cannot help thinking that Confucius is the greatest psychologist we have produced—he realised so clearly that human beings are afraid of death and that from this fear arises their hatred of growing old. So, as old age is inevitable, he tried to devise a method of making people enjoy it and forget their fear. That is why he teaches us to respect our elders, and his teaching has dominated our minds for more than 2,000 years. We are now simply accustomed to being complimented on "becoming older," and it gives us happiness to feel that we are honoured and respected in age. Once Confucius was questioned by one of his disciples about "death," but he answered that he did not yet know life, so how could he know death. According to his teaching we have to worship our ancestors, and so as people grow older they know that there will be younger generations to respect them alive and worship them after death, and the fear of death diminishes: we do not let it ferment our minds at all.

Our family system is largely based upon service for the older members—we have to serve parents and grandparents filially and to bring up the next generation so that they in turn will serve us. Nobody minds working hard for the first part of his life if he knows he will be able to enjoy his old age. Everybody has less vitality as he grows older and has to be looked after to some extent, but if there is a younger generation following, then there is no need to worry. If not, then old age must also be a worrying thought. Probably this is one of the Londoner's main problems. Also, as regards mothers I have been told that according to the English habit, if the father dies and leaves no will, the mother has to leave the house and find a new place to stay when her eldest son marries, because the house naturally becomes the property of the son. I was terribly shocked when I learnt this. Probably most English mothers are so familiar with the idea that they accept it as a natural course without thinking, but it seems to me horrible that the mother who has spent half a lifetime in bringing the son up should be turned out of the house where she has lived so long and where there are so many things she cares for. It is quite unimaginable to my sense of humanity, for though we may not be very grateful to our parents for bringing us into the world, yet they have done their duty for us in training and education. A mother may be glad to leave the old house and may hope to have more freedom and joy by herself, if she has enough money to find an even better house to live in. But from my way of thinking, she will not be so well-looked after by highly paid strangers when she is old and feeble as she would be by her own sons and daughters. In China a man has always sacrificed high posts and honours for the purpose of serving his ill and aged mother. Of course there are many questions to be discussed concerning our family system, which I cannot clarify entirely here, but somehow I feel that most Western women cannot be at rest all their life long until death comes. So it is natural that they have to worry more about being old than we do. It is well known in the West that a mother-in-law is a giggle-goggle for comedians. I dare say it is the same in my country, and perhaps we have even worse types, but as we are born with the idea of respecting our elders, we think we are bound to serve them, whatever their character, and make no bones about it.

My remarks will perhaps lead Westerners to think that we have so great a barrier between old and young that they can never mix together. But I think we may even be happier when our old and young people mix together, because we have no thought of age in a happy gathering at all. That is to say, the old will have no fear of being offended by being called old and the young do not show any pride in being young. I remember very well that my grandmother used to come up to our garden to have a look round when my brother or sister had gathered some of their friends there. She always smiled very happily when she came, and said: "Ah ha! you are here. Have you all got enough to eat and drink and amuse yourselves with? I can get you anything you want. I hope you are happy here and will have great fun this afternoon. Ah ha! . . .' Then she might chat a little bit to some of those present. As we all knew that she appreciated wine, sometimes she was offered several small Chinese wine-cups by the youngsters, as a gesture of respect. After she finished each cup, there would be a cheer and laughter. She might tease this and that young fellow, telling him for instance he would marry soon. Afterwards she would say again: "I must leave you all here now, because you will not be happy with an old nuisance like me around. I must go and try to get companions of my own age to play with. Ha ha!" Sometimes she brought many of her aged friends to play games with us youngsters. I never felt there was a barrier between old and young in my own experience. However, I would like to emphasise my point—that I am not asking my English friends to feel that to be old is a good thing; I only want them not to be offended if I happen to say "you are growing older," for that would be a compliment to me. I know the saying, "In Rome do as Romans do," but I sometimes speak without thinking. Oh, I have always longed to have a long white beard and bald head!

Though we do not mind becoming old in the natural course of events, yet we do desire to have a long life. There are plenty of things which symbolise longevity in Chinese art. And we have many stories about those who look for the secret of immortality. In about the second century A.D. there was an emperor, who thought that he had made the whole empire peaceful and prosperous. As he was an emperor he could get anything he liked, but he was grieved that natural laws forbade him to live beyond a certain age. So he tried to seek long life, and asked many priests and so-called immortals to be his advisers. Some of them had devised a special drug or pill which would keep a person alive a great number of years if he ate it. The preparation of it needed a long time and very expensive materials, so I suppose only an emperor could afford it. As soon as it was ready, it was kept in a hall of the palace, under the emperor's order: "Anyone who dares to take it shall be put to death." But one of his great ministers, called Tung Fang-Sho, the greatest humorist in Chinese history, came into the hall to steal it and ate it. Naturally, when he was found out he had to be executed. While he was going to the place of execution he laughed louder and louder, until the emperor heard him and made an inquiry. There-upon he said that there was no truth in that drug, be-cause it was said that he who ate it would live long. And

Tung Fang-Sho

now he had eaten it, but his death was upon him sooner than ever. Then the emperor sighed and released him, because he realised that "longevity" could not be found at will. Once I read of a well-known scholar who had written the following prescription for long life: two portions of patience, two portions of honesty, two portions of no-worry, and three portions of self-content with one portion of good wine to blend them all. I wonder whether he had worked it out well or not. However, anyone would be glad to have the one portion of good wine! Though I shall grow old before long, yet I can imagine now that there is a joy in being really old. I would like to conclude this topic by quoting a Chinese poem by Chu Tun-Ju (1080–1175):

> *I am happy with old age:*
> *For I have seen life thoroughly,*
> *Become familiar with all truths,*
> *Penetrated the hidden things of the world;*
> *Obliterated altogether the seas of regret and mountains of*
>   *distress;*
> *Free from the charm of flowers,*
> *And the spell of wine,*
> *Always sober.*
> *When I have eaten, I go to bed;*
> *When I awake, I play my part when my turn comes.*
>
> *Do not talk of the days gone by and time to come;*
> *In my breast*
> *There are no such things.*
> *I have no mind to become an Immortal, to worship Buddha,*
> *Nor to imitate the restless Confucius.*
> *I am unwilling to argue with you,*
> *Laugh as you will—*
> *So, be it so.*
> *My part performed,*
> *I leave my costumes to the silly players.*[1]

[1] Translated by Ch'u Ta-Kao.

Some Personalities

Here and there in the previous chapters, I have mentioned friends in London and some of them I would like now to describe more closely, as a sign both of gratitude and of admiration. As I do not often go to parties, meetings, and clubs, I may have missed a lot of chances to make friends, and though I like to attend good public lectures given by experts, yet I cannot easily express my admiration to them on such an occasion. However, real friendship is not often formed in these ways and more often arises from some unforeseen incident and it grows and lasts because of similar tastes and nature.

Sir James Stewart Lockhart and Sir Reginald F. Johnston were both well-known scholars and specialists in Chinese studies. Through the former, I was recommended to teach my mother tongue in the School of Oriental Studies. With the latter, I had always good talks on Chinese literature and poetry in the school. He was the head of the department of Far East there, and a great lover of mountains and rivers which are so much praised by our men of letters. He had a greater mastery of our language than any other English person I can name at the present day, so that we could sometimes talk in Chinese, as some poetic expressions are not really translatable. I used to visit Sir James every Saturday morning, for he always had something to discuss with me about Chinese texts and never stopped reading them even though he was about eighty. I liked his strong sense of humour. I am always inclined to think that a man of great personality with profound learning and knowledge is always eager to know something more and seems to make fun of his own ignorance, and to have a genuine sense of humour. But on the other hand, a narrow-minded person is always proud of his or her own knowledge and thinks nobody else has learned so much, so naturally he or she is often beset by trouble and jealousy. At my age I am just beginning to learn. When I was in China I used to wonder how I could ever get to the end of my studies, as big as an ocean, in Chinese. Now that I am in London and realise more and more about the world, my wonder increases, and these two great friends have told me that I shall have to keep on learning and studying without cessation even when I reach a fine old age. Now they have both died not very long ago and I have to leave the school too, after four years teaching there. This will be a page of my life history finished, and I am going to begin a real life study in memory of them.

I knew Roger Fry only slightly, but my acquaintance with him and my impression are always fresh in my mind. First Mr. W. W. Winkworth arranged for a well-known artist of my country to meet him at the National Gallery and I was allowed to accompany them. When we arrived, he was sitting in front of Rembrandt's self-portrait, copying it. He turned round to us with a very friendly smile and we shook hands. My friend knew French well, not English, so they talked together in that language. Then he turned over page after page of a book of reproductions of my friend's work and suddenly stopped at a horse-drawing, remarking "I like that." I was impressed by the sympathetic way he looked at that drawing because I was fond of it too. Though I did not talk to him at all while we were in the Gallery, I studied his face and movements again and again. Actually he only murmured a few words to my friend, and for most of the time we stood there very quietly and there seemed to be between us an understanding beyond words. Oh, this is one of the greatest moments I have ever experienced! I always think that a sense of real understanding does not lie on the surface and cannot just be interpreted by commonplace words, so it is often better not to say anything. At that time we were all looking at the self-portrait of Rembrandt which he was copying and had not yet finished. He pointed out how he could not get this and that part right, yet I felt the greatness in the self-portrait and in his own expression. I had always liked to look at this self-portrait of Rembrandt whenever I went to the National Gallery, because apart from the highly skilful craftsmanship of the artist in the colouring and brushwork, it reflected to me a man of great determination and deep devotion to his art despite all sorts of difficulties which he had to pass through and which were apparent in the wrinkles and lines of the face. After having read a little more about the life of Rembrandt, I began to understand why I was moved by this painting on first seeing it. I have seen many a portrait in London galleries, but never felt the same way about it. Roger Fry's own face did not stand out from that of many other English people whom I have seen in London. I did not feel any difference until I looked at him again and again while he talked to my friend. He had a usual type of face with wide forehead and two heavy lines under the cheekbone, into which I read the difficulties he must have overcome to carry out his determined purpose. Moreover, I felt his eyes had a special power of penetrating into the thing he saw. This is probably why he observed beauty in modern French art of the last century earlier than any other English person, though he met great opposition at the time, as I was told. Now visitors to the National and Tate Galleries enjoy looking at the modern works of art largely through his enlightened criticism. After standing in the Gallery for a little time, we had to leave him, but he said that we must go to his house one day. We fixed a date. When we got to his house, he let us in and took us directly to see different objects of art in his collection one after the other. There were several examples of Chinese art and he showed a great passion for them. My Chinese artist friend was not in favour of modern French art, though he studied art in Paris for many years, so he did not pass many comments when we examined those paintings. I did not utter a word from the beginning until I left, but I felt very keenly the atmosphere of a great English man of letters in that house. Although the place was not very big, yet it represented to me a positive palace of learning, beauty, and art arranged with an inspired order! Next time I saw him, it was again in the National Gallery and he was doing the same work as before. He beckoned me near him and said he had got one brush-stroke right. I thought I ought not to disturb his work and went away. The third occasion I saw him there too, but we only waved hands to each other. A short time later, his death was announced in the paper. I cannot express how much I was affected, and I always feel he is still alive somewhere in London and that he probably goes to the National Gallery sometimes. He was one of the greatest art critics of his day, but though a critic, he practised as well. Not only penetrating into the beauty of modern art, he loved a great deal in the old too, as he showed in his diligent copying of the Rembrandt portrait. He had also a wide knowledge and wrote much by way of introducing the art of my country to the West. Thus he has taught me to be broad minded and to enjoy beauty in any true work of art. I know many of my fellow human beings cannot get away from prejudice like the artist friend I mentioned, but I think one ought to open one's eyes wider in judging things. A real work of art will stand for ever, in spite of any detriment from individual prejudice! So Roger Fry is always alive and stands apart from his opponents whom nobody now remembers.

Before I came over here, I only knew that Mr. Laurence Binyon was the keeper of Chinese art in the British Museum and had written several books to introduce our paintings especially to this land. I had my first contact with him when I followed two friends of my country to visit the print and drawing departments in the museum. We were taken down to the basement and Mr. Binyon was there awaiting us. He only uttered a few words to us, but his calm, meditative eyes were arresting. We unrolled some good Chinese paintings, hung them up and rolled them up again, but he remained silent all the time. After we got out, one of us said that he had too much English reserve in his face which perhaps kept people at a distance. I was interested in this remark and wondered whether he would enter into conversation if other visitors wanted any explanations. That was five years ago. Since then, I have heard of him often, as he is the greatest authority on Chinese art in this country and I am very much interested in this subject too. After seeing many collections of Chinese art in different places, I realise his greatness in not saying anything when he showed us the pieces. He was simply telling us that we should look, not listen! In his writings and lectures he gives the readers and audiences a very clear understanding and appreciation of the subject, and I think he is the most skilful of all Englishmen in visualising what his own compatriots may best understand with the help of his literary talent. We Chinese thank him profoundly for his efforts to bring both countries into understanding of one another in some way on the cultural side, and I always believe that we shall understand each other thoroughly in the long run. The first person to make this effort should always be remembered. I have had many contacts with Mr. Binyon, but we have never talked very much. I am particularly interested in watching him when he gives lectures. I tried to make a cartoon of him when he talked on the subject of "Chinese Art and Buddhism." At that time, I sat amidst a big crowd, but only felt that I was in a Chinese temple. So I drew him in monk's clothes and his meditative eyes moved me to think of the very deepest aspects of our Buddhism! Only a little while ago, I asked him to give me five minutes to make a sketch of him and we talked a little more than usual. I said that he would have his tranquillity now after his retirement, but he replied, "No, people always want me to do something." After I finished the sketch, he showed me a self-portrait made when he was sixteen years old, and remarked that he could not paint. I wondered to myself why most great persons always seem more modest than any youngster. Afterwards a Swedish friend of mine saw the sketch and recognised him at once, and said that his face was more or less like that of English clerics, but I think his boundless knowledge was shown in it above all.

Mr. Eumorfopoulos' collection of Chinese art is known to the whole country as well as to us Chinese. I have had several contacts with him and he is always in my eyes a man with extraordinarily keen interest in the thing he loves. During the Exhibition of Chinese Art at Burlington House three years ago, I gave a series of lectures on "The principles and technique of Chinese calligraphy and painting" at the School of Oriental Studies, and he was a member of my audience. He paid for the course and never failed to attend as well as many other elderly people. At first, I felt embarrassed at being a young lecturer in front of many elders, as I was brought up in the principles of Confucius. I thought I could only answer their questions about Chinese art if they were to ask me, but hardly stand in such a prominent position and give instruction. This was a natural feeling in my heart, but of course the subject and circumstances made a difference as I was a native of the country which produced the art we were discussing, and I might therefore know a little more than those living in other countries. However, his presence at my lectures encouraged me very much in delivering the material carefully and enthusiastically. He has been collecting works of art for nearly half a century and it seems to me that he never stops collecting them as well as learning all about them. He does not confine himself to collecting old objects only, but modern ones too, which shows his keen interest in works of art for themselves, not merely in their antiquity. Once I took a group of friends round the exhibition, especially to examine the paintings. We talked more than two hours and he was always close beside me and never got tired. After many had gone and it was nearly closing time, he pointed out to me that he did not at first like the slightly coloured, misty landscape by Mi Fei of Sung dynasty, and now looking at it more and more he liked it very much. At that time, I could not express my great appreciation of his words and admiration of his desire to know everything thoroughly. I wonder how many collectors are as keen in their interest and how many would not be prejudiced by their own knowledge of the subjects already in their collections. Oh, there is no end to learning! There is no time limit for comprehending the great works of art! Furthermore, there is no boundary to the art that may still be created in the world! I wish all the men of power in the world could follow the example of good collectors of art whose own collection helps them to appreciate others while the men of strength with their collection of intellectuals always try to destroy others. Mr. Eumorfopoulos is an example to be set up to the world for a lover of art. I am grateful to have known him.

I do not know how and when I got to know Mr. Herbert Read. I remember I was told that he lived as a hermit in London and very seldom talked. At that time, I was very much intrigued to know of "a hermit in London" because our conception of such a person is that of a man who generally lives in the mountains and is disgusted with town life, regarding it as a centre of vulgarity, quarrels, and troubles. But after all, to live in a town is not so bad as one thinks, so "a hermit in London" is not impossible! I met Mr. Read occasionally, when he lived at Church Road, now called Tasker Road, which was quite near where I stayed. Though he does not talk very much when we meet, yet I generally can read a lot of words he would say from his face. He weighs his words very carefully. When he looks at things, either big or small, I always feel he is in contemplation and he may put down his impression some time later. Once or twice, we happened to be at the same parties. I found him a little bit shyer than I was among a crowd. He talked even less than I did, because I was often asked "Where do you come from?" and "How do you like the English weather?" Of course nobody would ask *him* such questions. One night I went to see him and there were five of us there altogether. After a time three of us were left alone and if our third companion had not talked, we would have been completely in silence, because Mr. Read and I did not open our mouths. One morning we met at Belsize Park tube station because he was going to his office and I was going out too. He had a daily newspaper in his hand and I was just reading his latest book called *Art and Society*. I said to him that his new book was a great instruction to people who wanted to live in a society without art, and I liked the way in which the book was produced by Faber and Faber, apart from his beautiful style and thought. Then he turned over his newspaper and pointed out a photograph taken at Madrid and showing the courtyard of a church in which a statue of a saint had been wrecked by a bomb. The head of the statue was upside down in the mud, feet upwards. After a pause he said to me that was exactly like the surrealistic art. I agreed, but the thought rose also in my mind that the surrealistic work of art would become realistic after a number of years! How destructive the world is now! But art is always creative! Recently Mr. Read has moved to Beaconsfield and perhaps he is now enjoying a real hermitage.

After seeing a production of *Armlet of Jade* at the Westminster Theatre, I was interested to make the acquaintance of the Earl and Countess of Longford at Mr. S. I. Hsiung's. I know little about drama, so we did not talk much, but they impressed me deeply and seemed to contradict my preconceived idea of that type of person. A Chinese proverb says: "To hear a hundred times is not equal to seeing once." Later I met them a second time, when they produced *Yahoo* in London and came to see my exhibition of English lake drawings at Calmann Gallery. I felt honoured to be asked to stay in their house in Dublin and managed to do so last April. Before going I asked to be allowed to come without an evening suit, but when I arrived I realised that I need not have worried about the restraint of pomp and ceremony—I was particularly grateful that there was no uniformed servant to wait upon us at meals. I found them chiefly occupied in their main interest—the drama, and working very hard for it. Once I asked Lady Longford for some information about Bond

PLATE XVa. *The Earl of Longford*
(IN LORD LONGFORD'S COLLECTION)
PLATE XVb. *Sir William Milner*
(IN SIR WILLIAM MILNER'S COLLECTION)

Street and Regent Street, but she told me she very seldom went there. This was a great surprise to me, because I thought all ladies would know something about them, especially one of her rank. The Earl was busy getting together costumes for one of the plays at the Gate Theatre, of which he is the manager. I thought he might delegate this task to somebody else, but he preferred to do it himself. These two people are about the same age as I am and made me feel that I had accomplished very little in comparison. On my very first impression they struck me as being different from others, and now they have my great and continuous admiration for their industry, kindness, and interest in humanity. They refute my idea that people are apt to lose their better instincts when they are in a high position. On getting to know such people as Lord and Lady Longford my dislike of those of my fellow-countrymen who abuse their high positions in China increases. I think that all that my country has suffered for many years now is largely due to this type of person. We do not fear the enemy invasion, but we apprehend corruption from within among those who try to protect their own property and become pro-enemy. However, they are a very small minority of our vast population and their influence can be wiped out in time. I have a cousin who, as he does not belong to the direct line of my family, lives in another house. He is very rich and owns many houses, shops, and premises in my native city. Once a month he came to pay his respects to my grandparents and the first time I saw him, when I was about eight, he gave me several dollar notes to buy sweets and toys. I tore them all into small pieces in front of him, because I had heard so many stories about his laziness and selfishness and cruelty to his servants and tenants. I was of course reprimanded severely by my grandmother for being so rude, and she said I could simply refuse to accept it instead of tearing it into pieces. "With money you can move the gods; without it you can't move a man," says a Chinese proverb. But it would not apply to a stubborn child! I would like to thank Lord and Lady Longford for having taught me a great deal by their daily life.

Another friend whose interest in humanity has won my heart is Sir William Milner. A long time after the exhibition of my paintings at Betty Joel's Gallery in 1936, I had a letter from him asking if there was any possibility of seeing my paintings. He had been away during the exhibition, but had seen four of the paintings reproduced in the *Illustrated London News* while on board ship on his way back to London, and after much difficulty had found out my address. The trouble he had taken impressed me greatly. We made arrangements for him to come and see my paintings and at first I thought of him only as a man who loved Chinese art. Since then I have dined in his London house in Cheyne Row many a time and have eaten mulberries from the tree in his garden, said to have been planted in Queen Anne's time—hundreds of years ago. I have also spent peaceful days in his Yorkshire home, Parcevall Hall. He again is a proof of my belief that a good friendship usually arises from some accident, not through formal procedure. Besides his architectural work, he is very keen on gardening. Whenever I have talked with him I have always found he was trying to do something for others and to give help where he could. This is the best way to happiness, and seems to me what a human being is made for. When the war broke out in my country in July 1937, knowing how depressed I should be, he made me come and stay with him in Yorkshire and gave all his sympathy to my country—I prefer to say to humanity— encouraging me to carry on my work, since I could do no direct service to my country. But the contrast between the peaceful countryside of England and the horrors happening in my own land was too much for me and eventually I felt compelled to return to London. Sir William has tried hard to help me out of many difficulties since I first knew him. Though all foreigners must encounter troubles of all sorts, they are much easier to bear with good friends.

London faces at a Punch and Judy show

Conclusion

In the foregoing chapters I have described what I have seen and thought in London during these past five years. I should like to write a great deal more on such things as ghosts, colours, cats, and dogs, all of which have interested me too, but I must not keep my readers longer or they will be exhausted. So I am going to make a long pause, until perhaps after several more years in London I shall be able to draw further conclusions on what I have observed and thought. The more I look at London scenes the more friendly a feeling I have towards them. And the more I learn of the different phases of London life, the surer and deeper is my belief in humanity, love, and beauty. Why should people be separated by terms of race or nation?

London is now my second home. Since my college days I have never stayed anywhere in my own country for more than three years. I like travelling and hope to go on travelling all my life, but London will be my headquarters while I travel in Europe. Besides, these five years, during which London has shown me so much hospitality and entertained me in so many ways, will always be a good memory. I like to think that this book, which is like my claw-marks left on London slush by accident, as I said in the snow chapter, may perhaps not be so ephemeral as most claw-marks and may be seen by many people.

How strange is life, and how wonderful a human being can be! Had I not been born in this age of progress and destruction, fighting side by side, I should probably not have been able to see through life to the very bottom of human nature and hold my faith in its essential goodness. I cannot think that hatred really exists in mankind, in spite of all the evidence which tries to pervert my way of thinking. Between individual and individual there is no such thing. Why should not all we human beings open our eyes wider and try to see the other side? I owe to London's friendship, kindness, and faithfulness a particular debt, which I hope I shall find a way to repay.

By now my readers possibly doubt the truth of my name — the Silent Traveller. Surely I have not appeared to be silent at all! Without further explanation and without trying to compare myself with our great philosopher, Lao Tzu, who wrote *Tao-Te-Ching*, the well-known doctrine of Chinese Taoism, I should like to end by quoting about him the following poem, which was written by Po Chu-I of T'ang dynasty:

> *Those who speak know nothing;*
> *Those who know are silent.*
> *These words, as I am told,*
> *Were spoken by Lao-Tzu.*
> *If we are to believe that Lao-Tzu*
> *Was himself one who knew,*
> *How comes it that he wrote a book*
> *Of five thousand words?*[1]

[1] Translated by Arthur Waley.